THE WILDLIFE OF THE FOREST

A children's natural history of the Forest of Dean

Andy Seed

Illustrated by Kate Sheppard

Acknowledgements

A lot of people have given their time to this project, and I am extremely grateful for all the help I have received. In particular, I would like to thank the many wildlife experts and enthusiasts of the Forest who have shared their ideas and knowledge. A special mention must also go to Sue Middleton of Forestry England, who conceived the book and has been a marvel at bringing together all the elements that have made it possible.

Juliet Bailey

Kate Batt

Emily Bennett, RSPB

Henry Bond, Forestry England

Kevin Caster, Gloucestershire Wildlife Trust

Helen Chick, Forestry England

Leoni Dawson, Forestry England

David and Susan Dewsbury

Julie Godfrey, Forestry England

Rosie Kelsall, Gloucestershire Wildlife Trust

Gerry Meredith, Forestry England

Rick Mundy

David Priddis

Ben Robinson, Forestry England

Paul Rutter

Kate Wollen, Forestry England

Text © Andy Seed 2022;
illustrations © Kate Sheppard 2022

Editor: Simon Adams

Designers: Sarah and Noel Fountain,
fountaincreative.co.uk

Published by Foresters' Forest,
a National Lottery Heritage Funded
Landscape Partnership Programme.

All rights reserved. No part of this book may be reproduced, stored in a retrieval system, or transmitted in any form or by any means, electronic, mechanical, photocopying, recording, or otherwise, without the prior written permission of the publisher.

Contents

Introduction	4
Map of habitats to visit in the Forest of Dean	6
Main sections:	
Oak woods	8
Beech woods	18
Conifer woods	24
Meadows & pasture	32
Heathland	38
Rides, paths and roadside edges	44
Mining spoil heaps & quarries	52
Rivers & brooks	56
Bogs	64
Ponds & pools	68
Forest Biodiversity Projects	74
People who look after nature in the Forest	80
Native and non-native species	84
Sheep and grazing	86
Wildlife quizzes	87
The future of the Forest	90
Projects you can join	98
Answers	100
Image credits	102
About the author and illustrator	104

Introduction

A forest is much more than an area of trees. It is a living mosaic of habitats, a landscape that is home to deer, hawks, dung beetles, mottled butterflies, owls, foxes, newts, snakes and vivid flowers like the honeysuckle and foxglove. It is a place of delicate mosses and lichens, and fungi that recycle dead things so that the living can live.
It is a giant community of life.

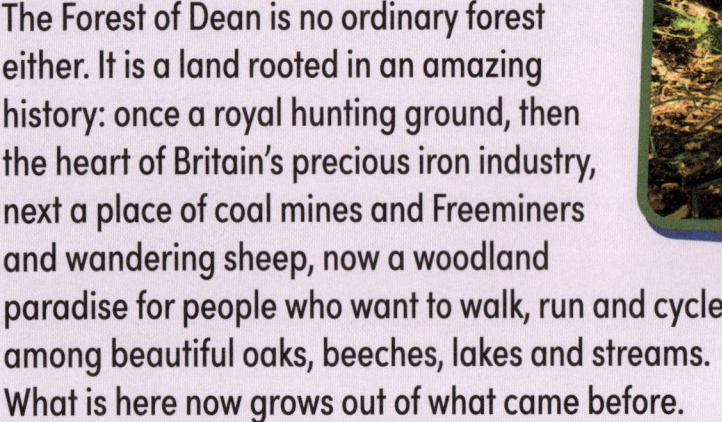

The Forest of Dean is no ordinary forest either. It is a land rooted in an amazing history: once a royal hunting ground, then the heart of Britain's precious iron industry, next a place of coal mines and Freeminers and wandering sheep, now a woodland paradise for people who want to walk, run and cycle among beautiful oaks, beeches, lakes and streams. What is here now grows out of what came before.

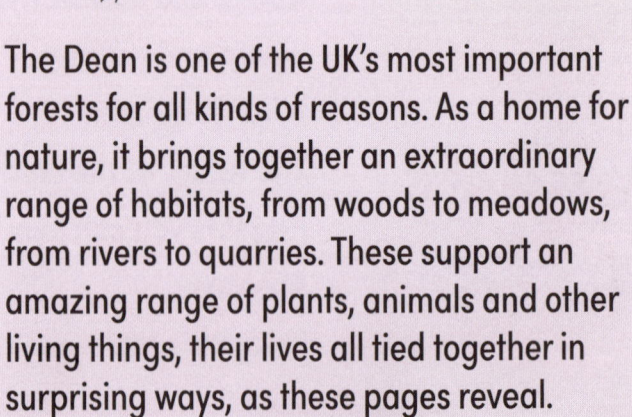

The Dean is one of the UK's most important forests for all kinds of reasons. As a home for nature, it brings together an extraordinary range of habitats, from woods to meadows, from rivers to quarries. These support an amazing range of plants, animals and other living things, their lives all tied together in surprising ways, as these pages reveal.

This book is an introduction to the wonderful wildlife of the Forest. It guides you through ten habitats and the wildlife you can find there. It describes some of the exciting projects going on to protect and help nature in the Forest and tells about the enormous challenges that the whole ecosystem faces in the future.

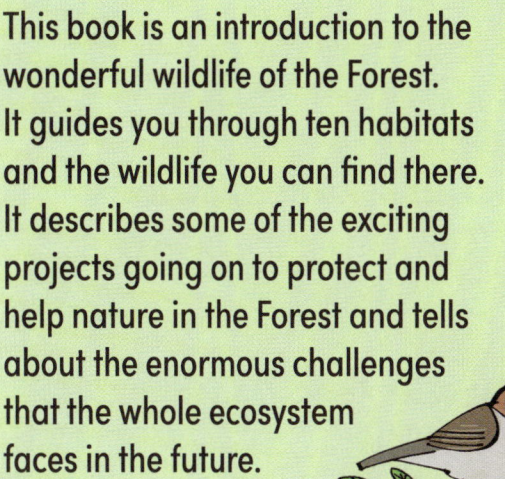

You'll also find wildlife-based puzzles to try and quizzes to do, and tricky questions to think about. I hope you learn a lot, and have fun doing it!

Andy Seed, February 2022

A few things to remember

1   The animals and plants listed in each habitat can be found in other Forest habitats too.
2   The best way to see lots of wildlife is to move quietly through the Forest – many animals have extra-good hearing!
3   To see even more, find a place to sit and keep still and silent for a while.
4   Early in the day and dusk (sunset) are often the best times to come across the rarer woodland creatures.
5   It's your Forest as much as anyone else's: look after it!

Oak Woods

Goat Moth

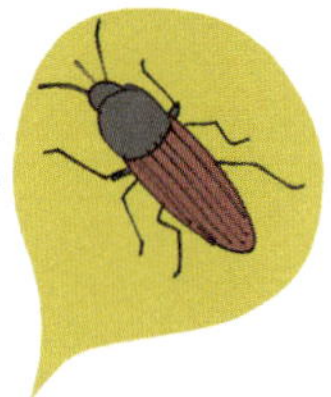

Oak Click Beetle

Lichen

Great Tit

The Forest of Dean is famous for its oak woodlands, and you'll never be too far from an oak tree if you venture into the woods. Many of the larger oaks were planted around 200 years ago to provide timber for shipbuilding, but were saved by the invention of stronger iron ships. Today, the oak woods are a key reason why there is such a range of wildlife in the Forest.

Green Woodpecker

Bechstein's Bat

Little Owl

Beefsteak Fungus

The oak tree

For centuries the oak has been the most important tree in the Forest. Its strong wood has always been highly valued for building as well as for making furniture and for fuel. Now the oak tree is also highly valued as a home for nature.

Oak facts

★ The oak supports more wildlife than any other tree in the UK
★ Some Forest oaks are 350 years old and these contain decaying wood which is food for huge numbers of insects such as beetles, as well as fungi and other living things
★ Acorns are a key food for boar, badgers, squirrels, wood mice and jays among others
★ Oaks planted close together grow straight and tall without low branches, and are less likely to become ancient trees

Oak numbers

70: the number of different gall wasps that depend on the oak
326: the total number of living things that depend on the oak in the UK
400: the typical age in years of an ancient oak (some live to be 800)
2,300: the total number of species supported by the oak
250,000: the approximate number of leaves on a large oak

One of the Forest's largest oaks

Look out for these

Great Spotted Woodpecker

A shy blackbird-sized woodpecker often seen clinging to tree trunks. It has a bouncing flight and a noisy sharp call.

How to recognise it
★ Black and white with red under the tail
★ Male has red patch on the head also

What it eats
Insects, spiders, nuts, seeds, eggs and young birds

Four facts
1. The woodpecker uses its strong beak to dig into trees to find grubs and also to make a nest hole

2. It has a long tongue (4cm longer than its beak) for reaching food
3. It drums on trees 10-16 times a second as a warning when marking its territory
4. It has a shock-absorbing skull

Treecreeper

This small, quiet bird spends its time hopping up tree trunks in a spiral movement. It is common in the Forest but not easy to spot because of its excellent camouflage.

How to recognise it
★ A small, round body
★ Mottled brown on top, white below
★ A thin curved beak

What it eats
Insects, spiders, and seeds

Four facts
1. Treecreepers have small territories, sometimes just one tree!
2. It weighs only 10g, about the same as a £1 coin
3. It uses its tail feathers as an aid when climbing trees
4. It is sometimes called the tree mouse

Nuthatch

Another small busy bird found on oaks, the nuthatch is quite common and easy to see.

How to recognise it
★ Plump, blue-grey on top
★ Creamy orange below
★ Short beak, short legs

What it eats
Insects, nuts, seeds

Four facts
1. It moves down trees head first (unlike the treecreeper, which flies down)
2. It hides nuts in tree bark as a food store
3. It often nests in old woodpecker holes
4. The nuthatch sometimes reduces the size of a nest hole entrance with mud to keep out squirrels and other intruders

Bluebell

You cannot miss the large 'carpets' of these pretty violet-blue flowers that appear across the Forest in April and May.

Bluebell basics
★ They grow from bulbs
★ Half of the world's wild bluebells are found in the UK
★ They are a sign of ancient woodland
★ Bluebell nectar is key food for bees and other Forest insects
★ They flower before the trees above them come into leaf, so their leaves can capture plenty of sunlight to make food
★ There are many myths and folk tales about them – one says that if you hear a bluebell ring you'll be visited by a bad fairy!

Herb Robert

These pretty little pink flowers are found all over the Forest and they supply nectar to insects such as bees. They have many nicknames including Stinking Bob (their leaves smell yucky if crushed) and the mysterious death-come-quickly. Herb Robert was once used as a cure for nosebleeds.

Oak moss lichen

This is not moss but a type of lichen that grows in clumps on the branches of oak trees. It looks like pale deer antlers and in some countries it is collected to make perfumes.

What are lichens?
Lichens are not plants but living things made up of algae and fungi existing together. They come in many colours and sizes and can be seen growing on trees, leaves, rocks and even earth.

What are algae and fungi?
Algae are a group of living things which are like plants without roots. Fungi are also living things which are not animals or plants – mushrooms and moulds are types of fungi.

Why are lichens interesting?
★ Like plants, they convert carbon dioxide (a gas that adds to global warming) to valuable oxygen
★ They can absorb pollution from the air (and help scientists study it)
★ They provide habitats for small creatures and nesting material for larger animals
★ Lichens grow on bare places such as rocks and logs, providing habitat for other creatures

Harder to spot

WOW wildlife — Wild Boar

Adults have dark, bristly hair while the young have lighter coats

The wild boar is a type of pig and a true native of the Forest, once hunted by kings and nobles. Boar became extinct from the UK around 700 years ago and are now back in the Dean having bred from animals which escaped from a farm or were illegally released in the 1990s and later. This means that the boar you see today are not truly wild but feral, which means they have learnt to live in the wild. They are exciting animals to see: big, strong and fast, although they are not popular with everyone, as you can read about below.

Boar background

★ Boar live in groups of adult females and young, called sounders, while the males live alone
★ Males are larger than females, and fight each other for the right to breed, using their prominent tusks
★ Females give birth to a litter of 6-10 piglets, often called humbugs because they are striped like the famous old sweets
★ Most wild pigs live for only 4-5 years
★ They have poor eyesight but very good hearing and sense of smell
★ There are more wild boar in the Forest of Dean than anywhere else in the UK; the best time to see them is at dusk

Boar jaw, showing the tusks

What do they eat?

Wild boar root through the ground with their strong snouts, searching for roots, bulbs, nuts and fruit although they eat almost anything edible they come across, including small mammals, worms, larvae, eggs and carrion (dead things).

Careful!
Boar normally run away with a snort if they notice you but females with young can be aggressive, especially towards dogs, so you may need to back off sometimes. It could be that the boar have an instinct to fear dogs because they are like the wolves which were once the pigs' only natural predator.

DO NOT FEED!
It is against the law to feed boar because this could lead to an outbreak of a deadly disease called African Swine Fever. The illness is not harmful to humans but it kills pigs and could lead to the Forest being closed.

Wild boar in the Forest today: the good the bad and the ugly

The boar which roam the Forest today are controversial animals because they do cause problems. People are divided in their views about the boar for many reasons. Here are some arguments for and against the boar. *What do you think?*

For	Against
★ They represent the return of a 'lost' native animal ★ They help to spread wild seeds ★ They keep down unwanted brambles and bracken ★ They bring visitors to the Forest who spend money at local shops etc.	★ Their digging for food damages gardens, playing fields, road verges, and farmland ★ They cause traffic accidents ★ They can damage habitats e.g. by eating the eggs of birds that nest on the ground ★ They damage fences.

Culling
Today's Forest boar have no natural predators and they breed rapidly, meaning that their numbers increase sharply if nothing is done. It is estimated that there were over 930 boar in the Forest in 2021. Forestry England would like to keep numbers at around 400 and so they employ wildlife rangers to cull the animals safely.

Be a detective

See if you can spot these five signs of wild boar around the Forest:

Footprints
Boar's feet are like deer hooves but rounder – you can see them in muddy areas

Rooting
Boar root up patches of ground with their snouts, looking for roots, grubs and other food

Wallows
The animals roll around in muddy clay pools like this to cool down or remove parasites from their skin

Scratching posts
Boar rub themselves on trees and poles leaving muddy marks

Droppings
Wild pig poo is lumpy, dark and not as smelly as you might think!

Redstart

A small bird which looks like a ninja robin! It flies to the UK each spring and leaves in September.

How to recognise it
- Long, red tail
- Male has black face and red chest
- Female brown and buff

What it eats
Insects, spiders, worms and berries

Four facts
1. Redstarts often bob when perched
2. They also make their tails quiver
3. Winters are spent in the warmer lands of Africa or Asia
4. They spend most of their time in trees looking for insects

Fallow deer

The most common deer in the Forest, these are larger than roe deer and can often be recognised by their short dark tails.

How to recognise it
- Gingery brown spotted coat (but can be darker)
- Male has large, broad antlers

What it eats
Young trees, bark, shoots, leaves, grass and other plants

Four facts
1. They often feed in glades and woodland edges in small groups, moving quickly into trees if disturbed
2. Numbers of fallow deer have to be controlled to prevent too much damage to young trees, and to keep the population healthy
3. Males do loud belly belches and fight in the breeding season to establish their territory
4. The deer were much prized by poachers during the Middle Ages

Roe deer

Smaller than the more common fallow deer, roe can be seen at woodland edges, especially around dawn or dusk.

How to recognise it
- Brown to grey, with a white patch on the rump
- No tail
- Males have short pointed antlers

What it eats
Tree buds, grass and other plants

Four facts
1. Less than 10% of Forest deer are native roes
2. Deer can destroy young trees so new plantations are sometimes fenced off
3. Females usually give birth to twin fawns which have spotted coats when young
4. Males fight in the mating season (July/August) then shed their antlers each October before growing a new set

Spotted longhorn beetle

This big, bright insect can best be seen at the edges of woodland. Also known as the black and yellow longhorn beetle, it appears in summer, especially in places where there are flowers to feed on.

How to recognise it
★ Black and yellow markings and spots
★ Long legs and antennae

What it eats
Adults feed on pollen and nectar; larvae eat rotting wood

Four facts
1. The beetle's eggs hatch into grubs which chew through tree stumps and old logs
2. It takes two or three years to develop into an adult beetle
3. Adults only live for 2-4 weeks
4. Like bees and other insects, this beetle helps plants and trees by spreading their pollen so they can reproduce

Silver washed fritillary

A big orange butterfly, speckled with brown, named after the streaks of silver underneath its wings.

How to recognise it
★ Male is a rusty orange with dark spots
★ Females are paler with bolder dark markings on the wings
★ Caterpillars are very spiky

What it eats
Adults feed on nectar of thistles and brambles in particular; larvae eat violets

Four facts
1. It sometimes eats honeydew, a sticky substance that aphids produce from their bottoms
2. Adults perform a spectacular courtship dance in the air
3. The male loops around the female then later sprinkles scented scales on her
4. The larvae hibernate under tree bark

Remember: Do not eat any wild fungus unless it has been picked by an expert.

Chicken of the woods

This strange-looking fungus is said by some people to taste like chicken. It's usually creamy yellow and grows on oaks or chestnut trees. Like many fungi, it's food for lots of insects as well as animals like deer.

Interesting characters

Jay
Another bird of the oak woods that avoids humans, the jay is a colourful member of the crow family with a brash, rasping call.

How to recognise it
★ Pale pink and brown, with black and white markings
★ Unusual blue barred wing feathers

What it eats
Acorns, seeds, berries, insects, eggs, small rodents and young birds

Four facts
1. The jay famously buries acorns as a food store and when forgotten these grow into oaks, helping to renew the forest
2. Some jays store over 2,000 acorns in the autumn
3. It can mimic the calls of other birds such as hawks
4. The parents work together to build a nest and feed their young

Woodcock
A pigeon-sized wader that lives in the woods, the woodcock is a mysterious and rarely seen bird.

How to recognise it
★ Very well camouflaged mottled brown body
★ Long straight beak

What it eats
Worms, beetles, snails, larvae

Four facts
1. A nocturnal bird, the woodcock hides during the day in undergrowth
2. It uses its long bill to probe the ground for juicy food like grubs
3. Males perform a noisy display flight, to attract a mate, from April to June
4. These birds have been hunted heavily for food in the past

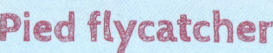

Pied flycatcher
Another small bird which visits the UK in the warmer months. The male and female have slightly different colouring.

How to recognise it
★ Male is black on top with white underneath
★ Female is mostly brown and white

What it eats
Insects such as flies, wasps, ants; caterpillars; fruit

Four facts
1. The pied flycatcher migrates from Africa each year, where it spends the winter
2. It is an agile bird, able to snatch insects in mid-air as well as on trees or the ground
3. The Forest of Dean is one of the best places to see it in the UK
4. It nests in tree holes

What is that?
Do you know what these things are?
Answers on page 100

A.

B.

C.

An oak wood food web

Every plant and animal in the Forest plays an important part in helping wildlife to survive. These are just some of the connections found in an oak wood:

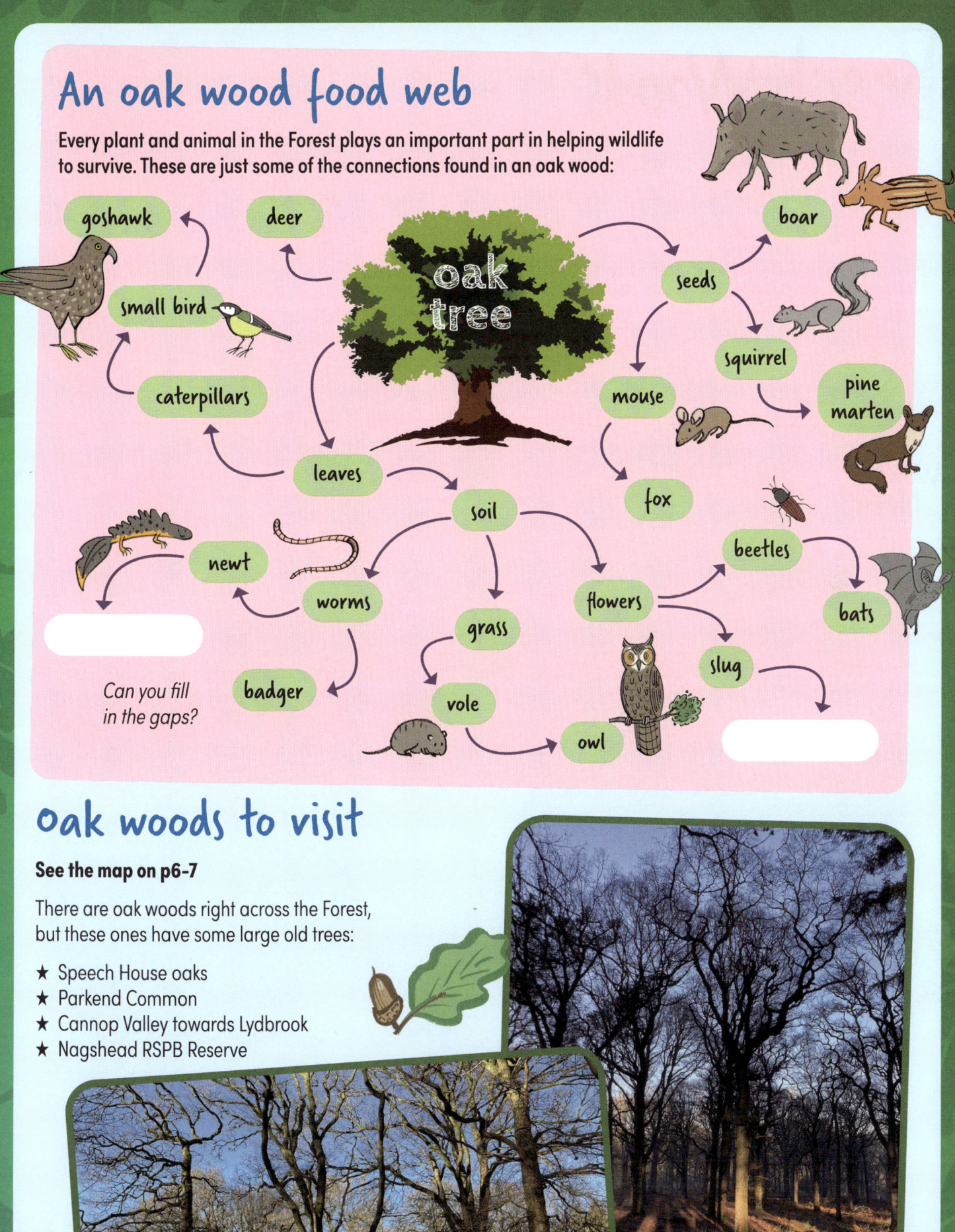

Can you fill in the gaps?

Oak woods to visit

See the map on p6-7

There are oak woods right across the Forest, but these ones have some large old trees:

★ Speech House oaks
★ Parkend Common
★ Cannop Valley towards Lydbrook
★ Nagshead RSPB Reserve

Beech Woods

It's usually easy to tell when you're in a beech wood because there is often little on the ground except a carpet of orange-brown leaves. Other plants struggle to grow under beeches because they block out so much light, but the trees themselves are home to many living things.

Bluebells

Wood Mouse

Vole

Porcelain fungus

Grey Squirrel

The beech tree

A beautiful and elegant tree, the beech produces a thick canopy of leaves which turn parts of the Forest vivid green each spring and then a rich copper each autumn. It can be recognised by its smooth grey bark.

Beech facts

★ Its new leaves appear hairy
★ In autumn its leaves can be green, yellow and orange-brown all at once!
★ The tree produces a big crop of seeds called beech nuts which are eaten by boar, squirrels, mice and birds
★ Young beeches are often damaged by squirrels stripping their bark

Good wood

Beech timber is much valued for all kinds of things including furniture, tool handles and for fuel logs. If you have a wooden spoon in the kitchen it's very likely to be beech wood.

Beech trees produce a wonderful display of colour in autumn

Look out for these

Grey squirrel

It may be cute but the very common grey squirrel is not popular with everyone as it does cause a lot of damage to trees, including the beech. It has also played a part in the loss of the native red squirrel from the Forest.

How to recognise it
★ Silver-grey fur, brownish face
★ Large bushy tail

What it eats
Bark, tree buds and flowers, berries, seeds, nuts, fungi, insects, mice, young birds, eggs

Four facts
1. It hoards food such as nuts by burying them in lots of places
2. Squirrels do not hibernate but stay warm in winter using their tail as a blanket
3. They have special feet which they can turn to move down a tree head first
4. It has few predators but pine martens have been brought to the Forest, and it is hoped these will help control numbers of squirrels

What did I do?
It may surprise you that the grey squirrel is classified as a pest. There are several reasons for this, but the problem was caused by this animal being introduced to the UK from its native North America in the 1800s. It spread very quickly and has caused a number of problems as an invasive species.

Grey squirrel challenges
★ They damage young trees by tearing off strips of bark and eating the layer of living wood beneath – this leads to stunted growth or even the death of the tree
★ They can outcompete the smaller red squirrel and also carry a virus fatal to reds
★ They breed very quickly and in large numbers have a negative effect on the balance of nature in Forest habitats

Squirrel damage to a beech tree

Woodland dor beetle

This stocky black beetle is a common sight on Forest paths and tracks. It's often seen lying on its back with legs wiggling, or crawling over dung in groups.

How to recognise it
★ Stocky black body, 12-20mm long
★ Metallic blue-black undersides

What it eats
Animal droppings

Four facts
1. Like many other dung beetles, it burrows under droppings then pulls the dung into the chamber to lay eggs in it (this also enriches the soil)
2. The larvae hatch and stay underground over winter, with the parents providing more poo to eat as needed!
3. Dor beetles have wings and can fly
4. Older beetles lose the ability to turn over, which is why many are seen lying helplessly on their backs

Black stone flower lichen

This grey-green lichen looks a bit like tiny seaweed. It is sensitive to pollution so only grows where the air is clean.

Harder to spot

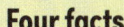

Tawny owl

Easy to hear but not so easy to see unless you are often out at dusk, this is the classic twit-twoo predator found right across the Forest.

How to recognise it
★ A rounded head and body, mottled brown
★ About wood-pigeon sized

What it eats
Voles, mice, small birds, frogs, insects and worms

Four facts
1. You can find owl pellets below their tree roosts – these contain undigested bones and fur of prey, coughed up in a small ball
2. Tawny owls prefer to nest in tree holes but they use old crow nests too
3. Pairs of owls hunt in territories, which they defend keenly
4. They swallow their prey whole

Wood warbler

A small, bright bird that arrives in summer and has an attractive song. It can be seen between May and August.

How to recognise it
★ Green upper parts with a yellow chest
★ White underneath

What it eats
Insects and spiders

Four facts
1. The wood warbler spends the winter in Africa
2. It migrates thousands of miles to the UK each year
3. It nests on or near the ground, often in a dome of dead leaves
4. It raises its head when singing in short, fast trills

Turkey tail fungus

This very common bracket fungus grows on both living and dead trees. Its shape and colour make it look like a turkey's tail. Like other fungi, it helps to recycle decaying material.

Bird's-nest orchid

This very strange, sickly-looking plant has no leaves. Instead, as a parasite it feeds off tree roots, especially from beeches. Its name comes from its own tangled roots, which look a bit like a bird's nest.

Some other forest fungi

These often have strange names:

★ Scarlet elf cup
★ Beefsteak fungus
★ Shaggy bracket
★ Horn of plenty
★ King Alfred's cakes
★ The sickener
★ Wood blewit
★ Stinkhorn
★ Plums and custard
★ Jelly ear

Be a detective

In beech woods and other Forest habitats you will come across small holes and the entrances to animals' burrows. See if you can work out which animal made these holes. Answers on page 100.

A.

B.

C.

D.

E.

Interesting characters

Hawfinch

A stocky bird with a large powerful bill. Shy and quite rare, it's most often seen in winter.

How to recognise it
★ Orange-brown head with very chunky bill
★ Looks quite cross!

What it eats
Seeds such as beech nuts, buds and shoots, insects

Four facts
1. Its strong beak can crush a cherry stone
2. It feeds high up in trees so is not easy to spot
3. The male bird chooses the nest site
4. Hawfinches like to keep their nests clean of poo

Beech woods to visit

See the map on p6-7

Patches of beech can be found all over the Forest. These locations have some of the best trees:

★ Edge End, between Lydbrook and Coleford
★ Bradley Hill Woods, (near Soudley),
★ Blakeney Hill
★ Around Dean Heritage Centre, Soudley

Hazel groves

Between the oak, beech and conifer woodlands of the Forest are patches of hazel trees. These small trees are rich in wildlife too, especially as they produce delicious nuts.

Hazel catkins

Hazel tree

These short bushy trees can be recognised by the many long thin stems that often grow from larger branches and in spring by its pretty hanging flowers called catkins. In autumn you may see hazelnuts growing in small clusters. These are much prized by squirrels and dormice as well as several birds including woodpeckers, nuthatches and jays. Its hairy leaves are eaten by many types of caterpillars.

Coppicing

If a hazel tree is cut back to near ground level it will produce lots of new stems which grow into long, bendy poles. This is called a coppice. For centuries these sticks have been used for building, fences, baskets and garden supports. Coppicing helps wildlife by allowing in more light for plants, which then increases insect numbers so providing food for birds and others. Coppiced trees can also live for hundreds of years.

Hazel dormouse

What a shame that these very cute small mammals are so hard to see! They live in coppiced woodland and have been badly affected by the loss of these habitats. Dormice are mainly nocturnal and like to stay well out of sight, often asleep.

How to recognise it
★ Golden brown fur
★ Big dark eyes
★ Long fluffy tail

What it eats
Nuts, seeds and berries in autumn, flowers and pollen in spring and insects in summer

Four facts
1. Hazel dormice hibernate under leaves and in small spaces on the ground, curled into a ball
2. Before winter they make a woven nest to keep their bodies warm
3. They are excellent climbers, with gripping pads and sharp claws in their feet
4. Predators include owls, weasels, foxes and boar (which find them hibernating by chance as they have no scent)

23

Conifer Woods

Many of the Forest's conifer woods are made up of tall trees, growing close together, and planted in neat rows, but they are not all like that. They are also home to more living things than you might think!

Wood Ants

Pine Marten

Crossbill

Firecrest

Muntjac deer

Conifers

Conifers are trees which grow cones (such as pine cones), which contain seeds. Conifers have needles instead of broad leaves and they keep these over winter, except for the larch tree.

Most conifers are good at surviving cold weather and they are useful for timber because many grow quickly and often tolerate poor soils. The softwood they produce is often used to make paper and cardboard, among many other things.

Douglas fir
★ A native of North America
★ It can grow very tall (up to 60m!)
★ Douglas firs grow well in the Forest

Norway spruce
★ A tall, narrow 'Christmas tree'
★ Produces long, narrow cones
★ Can suffer from squirrel damage

European larch
★ Sheds its needles each year (a deciduous tree)
★ Turns an attractive gold colour in autumn
★ Has small cones
★ Produces valuable timber

Tree killer
Many areas of larch and chestnut trees across the Forest have been cut down recently to try and stop the spread of a disease called phytophthora ramorum which can be deadly to these species (see page 91).

Know your cones
Can you tell which is which: spruce, larch, pine and fir?
Answers on page 100.

Tree words
Coniferous: has needles and cones
Deciduous: drops its leaves
Broadleaved: has flat leaves, not needles

More conifers
You can also see these trees growing in the Forest:

★ Scots pine
★ Yew
★ Western hemlock
★ Corsican pine
★ Sitka spruce
★ Lawson cypress
★ Western red cedar
★ Wellingtonia
★ Redwood

Look out for these

Siskin

A busy little forest bird which is like the greenfinch but has more of a stripy body. Look out for its forked tail.

How to recognise it
★ Male has a streaked yellow body and black crown on the head
★ Female is a lighter greenish-yellow with no crown

What it eats
Tree seeds and some insects

Four facts
1. Siskins sometimes gather in noisy groups to feed
2. They often visit garden bird feeders in winter
3. The female builds a nest high in a conifer to avoid predators
4. Its call sounds like, "tilu, tilu"

Walnut orb spider

This is a common spider which creates a large, round web, often across branches at the edges of woodland.

How to recognise it
★ Dark brown, flat body
★ Wavy pattern on body

What it eats
Flies and other small creatures

Four facts
1. It hides during the day, often under bark, and emerges after dark to check for prey on its web
2. It builds a new web each night, eating the old one so the silk is not wasted
3. Females are larger than males
4. It is also known as the toad spider

Foxglove

You can't miss these tall pink-purple spikes that flower across the Forest in summer. They are an important source of nectar and pollen for bees but poisonous to humans, although they contain a chemical that can treat people with heart conditions. Foxgloves have many old names including dead men's bells and are sometimes called 'snompers' by Foresters.

Beard lichen

This harmless bushy lichen can be spotted on the branches of trees in damper areas. It only grows in places where the air is not polluted.

Harder to spot

WOW Goshawk wildlife

A large, powerful hawk which can sometimes be heard crashing through trees as it hunts at high speed. It is a very agile flyer with broad wings and long tail.

How to recognise it
★ Barred plumage with a grey head
★ Long yellow legs and red eyes
★ Larger than a sparrowhawk but slightly smaller than a buzzard

What it eats
Birds including pigeons and thrushes, squirrels and other small mammals

Four facts
1. Goshawks were once nearly extinct in the UK
2. They were often used by falconers in the Middle Ages
3. They perform a sky dance in winter to attract a mate
4. It is difficult to see them!

Firecrest

This tiny but attractive bird is the second-smallest in the UK. It is extremely rare but might be seen in winter flitting about looking for food.

How to recognise it
★ Bright green back, white belly
★ Female has yellow patch on head, male's is bright orange

What it eats
Spiders, small insects like aphids, moth eggs

Four facts
1. A firecrest weighs about the same as a 10p coin
2. The female lays up to 12 tiny eggs, just 12mm long
3. Its nest hangs on a branch suspended by cobwebs
4. Predators include sparrowhawks and squirrels, which sometimes eat nestlings

Crossbill

A chunky member of the finch family, this bird is famous for its special beak which it uses to get seeds out of pine cones.

How to recognise it
★ About sparrow-sized
★ The male is red, the female green
★ Its bill is crossed over at the tip

What it eats
Pine cone seeds

Four facts
1. Crossbills are hard to see because they spend a lot of time in treetops
2. It sometimes gathers in flocks
3. It nests earlier than most other birds in the Forest
4. Its special beak is used to force open tough pine cones so that the seeds can be removed

Southern wood ant

This is the largest ant found in the UK and is a powerful predator, living in large nests. Watch out because they also spray acid!

How to recognise it
★ Workers are red-brown
★ Look for dark heads and hairy bodies

What it eats
Invertebrates (e.g. insects, caterpillars, spiders) and honeydew from aphids

Four facts
1. Wood ants live in very large colonies of over 100,000 – watch out for their nests which look like big piles of pines needles or twigs
2. Each nest contains queens, males and female workers which will fire little jets of formic acid when threatened
3. Their main food source is a sweet, clear liquid that is actually a type of insect poo called honeydew
4. Predators include birds and badgers, which eat the ants' larvae and eggs

A wood ant nest

The return of the pine marten

In 2019 Project Pine Marten was launched locally as 18 of these impressive predators were released into the Forest of Dean in the hope they will breed. The pine marten is a mammal that was once common across the UK but has now become much rarer. It is expected that the animals will play an important part in the woodland ecosystem of the Forest, partly by reducing the number of squirrels. They are very hard to spot!

Champion hunter

★ The pine marten is an excellent climber and very agile hunter, about the size of a cat, with powerful claws and sharp teeth

★ Like other members of the weasel family, it has excellent eyesight, smell and hearing

★ Most prey is captured on the ground and includes voles, mice, birds and frogs but they also eat eggs, insects, fruit, berries and carrion

★ They inhabit tree holes or old squirrel nests and patrol an area of forest, leaving poo on stones and stumps to mark their territory

★ They are a protected animal and the Forest's martens are monitored by radio tracking and cameras

Interesting characters

Muntjac deer

These small, dog-sized animals are also sometimes called barking deer because of the loud repeated calls they make. They are found in oak and beech woods as well as conifers.

How to recognise it
★ Smaller than roe and fallow deer
★ Brown coat, slightly humped back
★ Males have short horn-like antlers

What it eats
All kinds of plants including young trees, bramble, honeysuckle and wild flowers

Four facts
1. Muntjac are native to China and were introduced to the UK
2. A number escaped from a deer park around 100 years ago and have now spread across woodlands such as the Forest
3. They can do a lot of damage to woodland and garden plants
4. Male muntjacs have long canine teeth like tusks

What is that?

Do you know what these things are? Answers on page 100.

A.

B.

C.

Be a detective

See if you can spot these five signs of deer around the Forest:

Footprints
These are called slots – this one is from a fallow deer. They are narrower than boar footprints

Wallows
At rutting (mating) time in autumn, fallow deer roll around in smelly mud and make loud grunts

Trails
Deer move around the Forest leaving tracks and slides where they drop down steep banks.

Fraying
Male bucks rub their antlers against trees to clean off the new 'velvet' (a kind of furry skin) and to mark their territory. This can damage young trees.

Droppings
Deer poo is made up of small, raisin-like pellets, usually dark and shiny.

Conifer woods to visit

See the map on p6-7

There are conifers all over the Forest, so they are not hard to find! You can see some interesting ones in these places:

★ Soudley Ponds
★ Redwood grove, near Soudley (for giant redwood trees)
★ Spruce Ride (near Speech House)
★ Woods beyond Cyril Hart Arboretum
★ Barn Hill (above Bixslade)

Meadows and Pasture

There are not many meadows among the trees of the Forest but around the edges of the woodlands are lots of small fields and patches of grassy land. These can be incredibly rich in wildlife, especially where wildflowers have been allowed to grow. Pasture is land grazed by animals such as sheep and ponies, and this is an important habitat too.

Buzzard

Cinnabar Moth

Large White Butterfly

Cowslip

Look out for these

Common buzzard

This large bird of prey can be seen and heard soaring over hillsides, both alone and in small groups. They can also be found in woodlands resting on branches but are easier to spot over open grassland.

How to recognise it
★ Big broad wings, dark at the tips
★ Wingspan of over one metre
★ Fanned tail

What it eats
Small mammals such as voles and rats, plus birds, carrion (dead animals) and insects

Four facts
1. It has a high-pitched piercing call, something like 'kee-yaa'
2. Females are larger than males
3. Buzzards build large nests in trees at the fork of two big branches
4. In flight they are sometimes mobbed by groups of crows who are keen to protect their young from predators

Cinnabar moth

If you see what looks like a red and black butterfly in open spaces around the Forest during the summer then it may well be the handsome cinnabar moth.

How to recognise it
★ Black and red wings with red spots and stripes
★ The caterpillar has tiger-like orange and black stripes

What it eats
The caterpillars eat mainly the ragwort plant, the adults feed on nectar.

Four facts
1. The moth's caterpillars feed on the toxic ragwort plants, making them poisonous to birds
2. If food is short the larvae sometimes turn into cannibals and eat each other
3. They fly in the daytime as well as at night
4. The moth has been introduced in some countries to control ragwort, which is toxic for horses and cattle

Large white butterfly

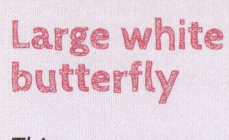

This very common insect is sometimes called the cabbage white because it lays its eggs on cabbages and similar plants for its very hungry caterpillars to devour.

How to recognise it
★ Large white wings with black tips, dark body
★ Females have spots on wings
★ Caterpillar is hairy with green, black and yellow markings

What it eats
Larvae eat brassicas (plants in the cabbage family), adults feed on nectar of wildflowers

Four facts
1. The female lays small yellow eggs in groups of 40-100 on leaves
2. Its caterpillars are toxic to predators
3. The caterpillars are attacked by a parasite, the ichneumon wasp, which lays its eggs on them. When these hatch the wasp's larvae eat the caterpillar from the inside.
4. There is also a very similar butterfly called the small white

Meadow grasshopper

This small jumping insect is easy to see in meadow grass and woodland edges during the summer.

How to recognise it
★ About 2cm
★ Green and brown

What it eats
Grass and other plants

Four facts
1. Unlike other grasshoppers, the meadow grasshopper cannot fly
2. Males make a churring noise by rubbing their legs against their wings
3. The sound is made to attract females
4. Young grasshoppers are called nymphs

Meadow wildflowers

The Forest's meadows are rich wildlife habitats. They are often bordered by hedges and trees which give cover to birds, mammals and other animals. The meadows themselves sometimes contain huge numbers of colourful wildflowers, usually best seen in May and June.

Adder's tongue

Orchids and other wild flowers in Clarke's Pool Meadow

Clarke's Pool Meadow

Just outside Blakeney is a traditional hay meadow which contains over 45,000 orchids in spring each year. It is a Site of Special Scientific Interest (SSSI) and also very beautiful!

Some meadow flowers found around the Forest
- ★ **Yellow rattle** (a parasite of grass and other plants)
- ★ **Mouse ear** (its leaves look like mice ears)
- ★ **Horsetail** (shaped a bit like a horse's tail)
- ★ **Fairy flax** (if eaten makes you run to the loo!)
- ★ **Adder's tongue** (a strange-looking green fern)
- ★ **Quaking grass** (has purple 'hearts' that quiver in the breeze)
- ★ **Lady's smock** (also known as the cuckooflower)
- ★ **Pignut** (with fat brown tuber roots, beloved of pigs)
- ★ **Goatsbeard** (also called Jack-go-to-bed-at-noon because its flowers close after midday)
- ★ **Yorkshire fog** (a soft, hairy grass with purple seed heads)

Why meadows matter
The UK has lost over 97% of its traditional wildflower meadows in the last 100 years. The few that are left are vital homes to all kinds of animals and plants. The plants feed the insects which in turn feed birds, bats and small mammals which in turn feed predators such as owls and foxes.

Meadow facts
- ★ Wildflowers grow best in poor soils. If fertiliser or richer soil is added, most flowers die and grass takes over.
- ★ Traditional meadows are cut to make hay in July
- ★ Some church cemeteries across the Forest act as wildflower meadows
- ★ You can make part of your garden lawn into a mini-meadow by joining in 'No-mow May' and continuing this into summer: bees and other animals will be very happy!

Dung beetles busy burying horse droppings

Poo is good!

The sheep, horses, cows and other animals that graze in meadows around the edges of the Forest produce a lot of droppings. This feeds flies, dung beetles and other living things which in turn feed predators. A dung beetle can smell a fresh cow pat from 2km away and when it flies over to tuck in, may be gobbled up by a bat or bird.

Quaking grass

Harder to spot

Barn owl

If you are out at dusk you might see this pale, ghostly hunter swooping over a meadow looking for small mammals in the grass.

How to recognise it
★ Light brown on top, white underneath
★ Light, heart-shaped face

What it eats
Mice, voles, rats, shrews and small birds.

Four facts
1. Barn owls sometimes hunt during the day in winter
2. They do not hoot but instead screech, hiss and even purr
3. Owls have an amazing sense of hearing: their main way of finding prey
4. They are in decline across the UK – one problem is a lack of nesting sites

Small pearl-bordered fritillary

This very rare butterfly is being protected in the Forest as part of a special project.

How to recognise it
★ Orange speckled, medium-sized, wings have a border of light 'pearls'
★ The caterpillar is dark with orange spots and short hairs

What it eats
The caterpillars feed on violets, the adults drink nectar from flowers such as buttercups, dandelions and thistles.

Four facts
1. The Forest is now the only place these butterflies breed in Gloucestershire
2. Its numbers have declined sharply due to the loss of damp wildflower habitats across the countryside
3. Some birds are predators of the adult butterflies
4. It flies close to the ground, sometimes gliding short distances

Waxcap fungi

This is a whole group of lovely brightly coloured mushrooms which appear in the autumn. They are often tiny fungi and can be found in wildflower meadows and pastures. They come in lots of colours, shapes and sizes.

Interesting characters

Mother Shipton moth

Mother Shipton was a famous old fortune teller from 500 years ago, sometimes called a witch. Amazingly this moth seems to have her face on its wings!

How to recognise it
★ Brown with cream markings and patterns that look like a creepy face with a big nose and chin
★ Wingspan is about 3cm

What it eats
The caterpillars eat clover, other flowers and some grasses; the adults search for nectar

Four facts
1. This day-flying moth can be seen in May, June and July
2. Its dull yellow larvae sometimes stand up on short legs
3. It hibernates as a pupa among grass
4. Mother Shipton was not great at predicting the future: she said the world would end in 1881!

A simple meadow food web

Animals in an ecosystem depend on each other and on plants to survive

Meadows to visit

See the map on p6-7

These are all worth visiting, especially in late spring and early summer when wildflowers are in bloom:

★ Worcester Walk, near Broadwell
★ Angus Buchanan Fields, Coleford
★ Clarkes Pool Meadow, near Blakeney
★ Ridley Bottom, near Tidenham
★ Ruspidge Halt (previously Linear Park Cinderford)
★ St Briavels Common
★ Wye Valley

Heathlands

Common Blue

Common Lizard

Nightjar

Green Tiger Beetle

Golden-ringed Dragonfly

Stonechat

Heathland is very different from woodland habitat. It is open space, with only the occasional tree, covered in tough plants like heather, spiky gorse and rough grasses. The Forest's heathland areas are not large, and some were once industrial sites, now being recreated as wild places. They can be very dry in summer and very wet in winter, with lots of ponds or ditches. As a result, they feature all kinds of interesting creatures.

Woorgreens, near Speech House, includes areas of heathland as well as a lake

Woorgreens in autumn

Look out for these

Common blue
A lovely sight on a summer's day, the adult flies around looking for yellow birdsfoot trefoil plants.

How to recognise it
★ Males are bright blue with white-edged wings, females more brown
★ Underwings are speckled

What it eats
Adults feed on nectar; caterpillars eat trefoil and clover leaves

Four facts
1. Its eggs look like tiny sea urchins, smaller than 1mm
2. Its caterpillars make sticky honeydew which ants eat
3. They also give off chemicals which cause ants to protect them
4. The caterpillars produce fine silk threads which are used to make a cocoon for the next stage of transformation into an adult

Stonechat
If you walk across heathland areas in the Forest you may hear a sharp call that sounds like two stones being tapped together. This is made by the stonechat, a sparrow-sized bird with a short tail.

How to recognise it
★ Males have a black head with a rust-coloured chest
★ Females have a brown head and lighter chest

What it eats
Insects, spiders, seeds, berries

Four facts
1. The stonechat has a habit of flicking its wings together when sitting on a perch
2. It will make its alarm call when people are near
3. It nests in bushes close to the ground
4. Parents can sometimes raise two or even three broods of young a year

Common lizard
A speedy little reptile which can be spotted basking in the warm sun on logs or stones. It's also found in woodland glades and forest edges, where it scurries away from dangers.

How to recognise it
★ 10-15cm with long tail and scaly skin
★ Different shades of brown to green
★ Lined pattern of spots on its back

What it eats
Insects, spiders and slugs

Four facts
1. It can shed its tail if attacked (and grow a new one)
2. The female gives birth to 4-10 live young in July
3. Adults hibernate under logs and rocks, October-March
4. Predators include birds of prey, crows, foxes and cats

Golden-ringed dragonfly

The UK's longest dragonfly is a black and yellow killer, darting around looking for other insects to grab.

How to recognise it
★ 8cm long
★ Black and yellow bands
★ Green eyes

What it eats
Damselflies, butterflies, bees, wasps, beetles

Four facts
1. The dragonfly's larvae live in streams for up to five years before they climb out and transform into flying adults
2. The golden-ringed occasionally eats other dragonflies
3. Like all dragonflies it is harmless to humans
4. As with many other wild creatures it is under threat from climate change and habitat loss

Birds-foot trefoil

This low-growing yellow flower is an important food plant for lots of butterflies and other insects. Its seed pods look like birds' feet and the plant is sometimes called 'eggs and bacon' or 'granny's toenails'!

Harder to spot

WOW wildlife — Adder

The UK's only venomous snake is found in open areas around the forest as well as woodland glades and grassy places. It is very shy and so hard to see, but if lucky you might spot one sunning itself to keep warm.

How to recognise it
★ Brown or silvery-grey
★ Dark zig-zag pattern along its back

What it eats
Voles, mice, frogs and occasionally birds and lizards (all prey is swallowed whole)

Four facts
1. Adders kill their prey using toxic venom delivered in a bite (don't worry, it's extremely rare for humans to be bitten, and an adder bite rarely makes people very poorly)
2. Like other reptiles they hibernate over winter in burrows or sheltered places
3. Males fight for the right to breed with females, who later give birth to up to 20 live young
4. Young adders are eaten by birds of prey and crows

Palmate newt

This is the Forest's most common newt and is found across open spaces as well as woodland edges.

How to recognise it
★ Small, very similar to the smooth newt but has no spots on the throat
★ Male has a stringy filament at the end of the tail in the breeding season
★ Yellowish belly

What it eats
Small invertebrates (creatures such as insects, spiders, slugs, worms)

Four facts
1. Females lay individual eggs in water, wrapping them up in the leaves of pond plants
2. They can live up to 12 years
3. Young newts are called efts
4. Adults hunt for frog tadpoles in spring

Interesting characters

Nightjar

This mysterious nocturnal bird is rarely seen, although you might hear its eerie song if you are out at dusk in open areas like Woorgreens.

How to recognise it
★ Mottled brown colours giving it amazing camouflage
★ Short beak, pointed wings, long tail
★ A little larger than a blackbird

What it eats
Moths, beetles, dragonflies

Four facts
1. There are many folk tales about the nightjar, and it has nicknames such as fern owl and goatsucker (based on the myth it suckles goats)
2. It visits the UK each summer from Africa
3. It has a silent flight and reflective eyes, like an owl
4. Females lay eggs on the ground rather than make a nest

Green tiger beetle

A ferocious predator of grasslands and heaths, this dazzling beetle can be seen scuttling about on sunny days from April to September.

How to recognise it
★ Metallic green body with cream spots
★ Moves very quickly
★ About 12mm long

What it eats
Spiders, ants, caterpillars

Four facts
1. It will often fly away if disturbed
2. It lays its eggs in sandy soil
3. When the larvae hatch, they grab and eat anything small that passes their burrow
4. The larvae are sometimes attacked by parasitic wasps that lay eggs in them, resulting in maggots which eat their hosts alive

Heathlands to visit

See the map on p6-7

Take some wellies if you're visiting in the colder months:

★ Wigpool, near Mitcheldean
★ Woorgreens, near Speech House
★ Edgehills, near Cinderford
★ The Park Nature Reserve, Tidenham Chase

A typical woodland ride

Speckled wood butterfly resting on a leaf

Autumn in the Forest

Look out for these

Fox

The fox is one of the Forest's largest predators, a type of wild dog which can most easily be spotted hurrying across roads and paths at dusk or dawn.

How to recognise it
★ Rusty red-brown coat
★ Large, bushy tail

What it eats
Voles, rats, mice, birds, squirrels, insects, worms, fruit

Four facts
1. Fox burrows or dens are built for raising cubs
2. The entrances are often under tree roots
3. Each animal guards a territory, marking it with sprays of urine
4. Foxes use a highly developed sense of smell and hearing to hunt

Brimstone

This large butterfly's vibrant colour makes it quite easy to recognise unless it lands and closes its wings, which look just like leaves.

How to recognise it
★ Male has lemon-yellow wings, females are pale green
★ Small spots on each wing

What it eats
Caterpillar eats buckthorn leaves; adults eat nectar

Four facts
1. The brimstone is one of the first butterflies to be seen in spring
2. Veins on its wings help hide it from predators
3. Adults hibernate in cold weather
4. The word butterfly may come from the brimstone's yellow colour

Long-tailed tit

This appealing bird is easy to recognise with its long tail. It often gathers in small, noisy flocks of 10-20 birds.

How to recognise it
★ Narrow tail as long as the body
★ Mainly black and white with pink or grey markings

What it eats
Insects (especially caterpillars), spiders, seeds when food is short

Four facts
1. The long-tailed tit builds a remarkable ball-shaped nest from moss and cobwebs, with lichen for camouflage, adding over 1,000 small feathers inside
2. The nest is stretchy, expanding as the young inside grow.
3. Despite the nest often being made in a spiky bush for protection, many are destroyed by predators
4. Adult and young birds huddle together outside when cold

Orange tip

The male orange tip is one of the easiest butterflies to recognise and often appears early in the year when there is a warm spring.

How to recognise it
- Male has white wings with orange tips on top, female black tips
- Mottled green and white underwings

What it eats
Caterpillar eats the leaves of several wild flowers; adults feed on nectar

Four facts
1. The bright colouring is a warning to predators that it will taste BAD!
2. The female checks possible plants to lay eggs on by tasting them with her feet
3. Single eggs are placed on different plants because the larvae are cannibals
4. Each caterpillar transforms into a pupa which looks like a thorn

Buff-tailed bumblebee

This large bee can be seen from March to August in places where plenty of flowers grow.

How to recognise it
- Yellow collar near head
- Light-coloured tail

What it eats
Nectar from flowers

Four facts
1. These bees nest underground in colonies of up to 600
2. The tails of workers are almost white but the queen's tail is a buff colour
3. Some flowers are too deep for the bee's tongue to reach inside so it will often bite a hole in the side of the flower to obtain the nectar.
4. Males cannot sting.

Bracken

In summer and autumn you cannot miss the feathery ferns which cover large parts of the Forest. This is bracken, a plant which spreads very quickly through underground stems. Its large, branched leaves unfurl in spring and the stems grow up to 2m tall. Bracken is poisonous to grazing animals like sheep but shelters wildlife and is eaten by some caterpillars.

Honeysuckle

This climbing plant, also known as woodbine, grows in forest edges. The long stems twine around trees and sometimes hang down in long woody loops. The creamy-pink flowers have an appealing scent and their nectar feeds butterflies, moths and other insects. Its red berries are toxic.

Old honeysuckle stems

Honeysuckle flowers are easy to recognise

Harder to spot

WOW wildlife — lesser Horseshoe Bat

This rare and highly protected bat roosts in old barns around the edges of woodland. Its name comes from the horseshoe shape of its nose. About a quarter of the UK's population is found around the Forest and Wye Valley.

How to recognise it
[Please note that it is against the law to approach or disturb these bats without a special licence]

★ Like other bats it only emerges at dusk and moves quickly so can be tricky to identify!
★ When roosting it hangs from ceilings and is about the size of a plum
★ Unlike some bats it flies close to the ground and avoids open spaces

What it eats
Insects such as midges, moths, beetles, wasps, plus spiders which it often snatches off leaves and branches while flying

Four facts
1. Adults weigh less than a 20p coin and can live up to 20 years
2. They shout ultrasonic sounds through their special nose, which acts like a mini-megaphone
3. They hibernate over winter in the Forest's many caves, tunnels and old mines
4. One small barn can accommodate as many as 800 roosting bats!

Amazing bats

Bats really are incredible animals. For a start there are over 2,000 types of bat worldwide, and it is thought that 1 in 4 of all mammals are bats!

The power of echo
Many bats, including those that live in the Forest of Dean, catch their food in mid-air using a remarkable system called echolocation to find where it is in the dark. They produce a series of very rapid high-pitched sounds (which humans cannot hear) then detect the echoes of these signals as they bounce off objects, including tiny insects in flight. Amazingly, some moths have developed the ability to jam these calls!

Soprano pipistrelle bat

Thank the bat
Tiny pipistrelle bats can catch and eat 3,000 midges a night – that's a lot of biting insects that are not going to be bothering us! To grab insects in mid-flight, bats have astonishing flying skills and their paper-thin skin wings allow them to be much more manoeuvrable than birds.

More Forest bat facts!

★ Bats can drop their body temperature to save energy in winter
★ Many bats die from food shortages when there is a cold spring
★ Bats are easily harmed by pollution such as chemicals used to treat wood in old buildings
★ Some bats' ears are so sensitive they can hear a ladybird walking on a leaf
★ They are not blind, and use eyesight to check how dark it is as dusk falls
★ Females usually have one baby per year which feeds on milk while young
★ Bat poo is a sign that you have bats in your loft or attic: it looks like tiny soft and dry sausages

Greater hoorseshoe bat

Brown long-eared bat

Red-headed cardinal beetle

A mini-hunter of the woodland edges, this colourful beetle can be seen during May and June.

How to recognise it
★ Orange-red with black legs
★ Long, knobbly antennae
★ About 1.5cm in length

What it eats
Small insects

Four facts
1. Like many insects, cardinal beetles can detect smells with their antennae
2. Their bright colours put off predators such as birds
3. The adults like to sun themselves on tree trunks
4. The larvae can be found under bark on rotting logs

Some other bats found in the Forest

★ Barbastelle (rare)
★ Bechstein's (rare)
★ Brown long-eared
★ Daubenton's
★ Greater horseshoe bat (rare)
★ Natterers
★ Noctule
★ Soprano pipistrelle
★ Whiskered

Noctule bat

The large noctule bat lives in old woodpecker holes around the Forest. It makes a sound as loud as a road drill (we're probably lucky we can't hear it!)

Fly agaric

This easily recognised fungus is the classic fairy toadstool. It's often found hidden among birch trees but is toxic so best not touched.

Interesting characters

Glow worm

It's a beetle not a worm but the female does glow, lighting up at night to attract a mate in June and July. They are lots of fun to spot.

How to recognise it
- ★ A faint greeny-yellow glow seen on leaves during summer nights
- ★ The female has a dark segmented body

What it eats
The larvae eat slugs and small snails

I wish I were a glow worm, a glow worm's never glum, 'cos how can you be grumpy when the sun shines out your bum!

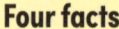

Glow worm in daylight

Four facts
1. Males do not glow but the insect's eggs and larvae sometimes do
2. The female cannot fly so climbs a plant before glowing in the dark
3. The light is caused by chemicals in the beetle's body
4. Adult glow worms live only a couple of weeks and die soon after mating and egg-laying

Wasp beetle

This clever insect looks and acts like a wasp to put off predators such as birds. It's actually harmless and doesn't have a sting.

How to recognise it
- ★ Black and yellow markings
- ★ Often found on logs and fallen branches
- ★ About 16mm long

What it eats
Pollen

Four facts
1. The beetle moves in a jerky fashion to mimic a wasp
2. It lays its eggs in dry logs or dead branches
3. The grubs (larvae) that hatch tunnel into the wood, like other 'woodworm', before emerging as adult beetles
4. Wasp beetles often fly away when approached

Be a detective

Animals often leave signs of feeding near paths. Can you work out what has been eating what here? Answers on page 100

A.

B.

C.

D.

E.

What is that?

Do you know what these things are? Answers on page 100

A.

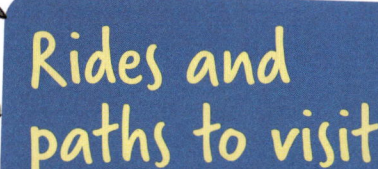

Rides and paths to visit

See the map on p6-7

There are thousands of rides, tracks and paths across the Forest to choose from. These are rich in interesting habitats:

★ Ruspidge Halt, near Cinderford
★ Awres Glow, from Mallards Pike heading north
★ Cannop Ponds
★ Russell's Inclosure

B.

C.

Quarries, Spoil Heaps & Mining

Redstart

Buddleia

Spleenwort

Raven

Grizzled Skipper Butterfly

For hundreds of years the Forest of Dean was a place of industry, with the land scarred by coal mines, iron works and quarries. There are still a few quarries among the woods, extracting blocks of pink and grey stone, but the big mines have all gone. Left behind are giant piles of unwanted material called spoil, huge holes in the ground, rock faces, and open spaces with remnants of buildings and machinery. Nature has gradually moved back into these places, as you will see here.

The Forest has hundreds of small quarries like this one near Broadwell

Look out for these

Raven

This large, intelligent bird of the crow family likes to nest on rocky cliff faces such as found in old quarries.

How to recognise it
★ All black with a slight sheen to the feathers
★ The tail is diamond-shaped in flight

What it eats
Carrion (dead animals) insects, berries, seeds, small animals, young birds, eggs, food waste

Four facts
1. Ravens mate for life
2. They defend a territory and guard their nest against predators
3. There are many myths about ravens and in some places they are regarded as a bad omen or a sign of death or evil
4. They are skilful fliers and put on acrobatic displays trying to impress others in the breeding season, even flipping upside down sometimes

Slow worm

This animal looks like a small snake but is actually a kind of legless lizard! It is the most easily seen reptile across the Forest, also found on heaths and grassy areas, often under logs.

How to recognise it
- Males are greyish, females brown
- It has a small head and smooth skin
- Looks a bit like a large worm

What it eats
Slugs, snails, spiders, worms

Four facts
1. Slow worms can blink (snakes cannot)
2. They are preyed on by adders, hedgehogs, badgers and birds
3. To put off predators it does stinky poos
4. If attacked it can also detach its tail, which continues to waggle!

Spleenwort

This is a type of fern which grows in tufts in cracks between rocks around the Forest. It was once used to make medicines for the spleen.

Buddleia

The 'butterfly bush' is a tough non-native shrub that springs up in rocky places and waste ground. Its fragrant purple flowers are attractive to many insects looking for nectar.

Harder to spot

Peregrine falcon

The world's fastest animal is a large powerful bird of prey. A good place to see them is the viewpoint on Symonds Yat Rock.

How to recognise it
- Long, pointed wings
- Blue-grey on top with a light barred chest below

What it eats
Birds such as pigeons, starlings and doves

Four facts
1. The peregrine can dive at 300kph to grab prey in the air
2. It strikes victims with its strong talons when diving, which is enough to kill or stun them
3. They nest on rocky ledges which is why they favour large quarries and cliffs, such as those along the Wye
4. Females are larger than males

Interesting characters

Crab spider

This eight-legged hunter looks like a small white crab. Amazingly, it can change colour gradually, so that it becomes camouflaged when hiding on a plant.

How to recognise it
★ White or yellowish
★ Crab-like appearance

What it eats
Bumblebees, butterflies, moths and other insects

Four facts
1. The crab spider does not spin a web
2. It ambushes insects landing on plants
3. Victims are grabbed then bitten
4. Its fangs inject venom which turn the prey's insides into liquid for the spider to drink

Grizzled skipper

This is a whizzy and well camouflaged little butterfly and also quite rare, so well done to you if you manage to spot one!

How to recognise it
★ Small and fast-flying
★ Brown with lighter 'checkerboard' patches

What it eats
Adults feed on nectar from flowers, larvae eat leaves of brambles and wild strawberries among other plants

Four facts
1. It likes to sunbathe on rocks or the ground
2. The male will chase others away from its territory
3. Grizzled skipper caterpillars make a silk shelter to feed under
4. The speedy adults are very difficult to follow!

What is that?

Do you know what these things are? Answers on page 100

A.

B.

C.

Quarries and old mining sites to visit

See the map on p6-7

There are many old mines and quarries across the Dean but take great care as some of them have dangerous drops. Keep away from fenced off areas and take note of warning signs. These are well worth a visit:

★ Stenders Quarry, Mitcheldean
★ Shakemantle Quarry, Ruspidge
★ New Fancy, near Moseley Green
★ Eastern United (off Staple Edge),
★ Waterloo screens near Mireystock

Rivers and Brooks

Water has played a major part in the story of the Forest's natural history. The Dean is bordered by two great tidal rivers, the Severn and the Wye, and it is crossed by a network of brooks, some fed by ponds and bogs. These streams tumble down hillsides and through valleys, carrying water that is mostly clean and full of life, attracting predators of all kinds. The larger animals also visit to drink, so the Forest's waterways are important wildlife habitats.

Blackpool Brook, a typical Forest stream

Look out for these

Kingfisher

One of the most appealing birds anywhere, the shy kingfisher is unmistakable as it darts over water with a brilliant flash of colour.

How to recognise it
★ Small with bright 'electric' blue on top and orange below
★ Long beak, white throat

What it eats
Small fish, water insects and tadpoles, which it dives into rivers to snatch

Four facts
1. There are over 100 types of kingfisher across the world but only one found in the UK
2. Fish caught are whacked on a branch to stun them, then swallowed head-first
3. It nests in riverbank burrows up to one metre deep
4. Kingfishers struggle to find food in harsh winters

Dipper

A plump bird which bobs up and down when perched on rocks. It likes fast-flowing streams with clear water.

How to recognise it
★ White throat with a dark body
★ Walks into water, going under to find food

What it eats
Insect larvae on riverbeds, freshwater shrimps, fish eggs

Four facts
1. It has special transparent eyelids so it can see underwater
2. Most birds have hollow bones but some of the dipper's are solid, to help it submerge
3. Dippers can stay underwater for 30 seconds
4. They are very sensitive to water pollution

Green shield bug

This common insect is well camouflaged, and is often found lurking on hazel leaves.

How to recognise it
★ A flat, shield-shaped body
★ Green with small spots

What it eats
Sap from plants which they suck out with sharp mouth parts

Four facts
1. It is also known as the stink bug because it produces a bad pong if disturbed
2. It changes colour in autumn to match the leaves
3. Shield bugs hibernate, emerging in May
4. Its eggs look like tiny grapes

Wild garlic

If you walk along streams in early spring you might notice a smell something like onions. This is from wild garlic, a plant that often grows near water and in damp, shady woods. It produces an attractive carpet of broad pointed leaves and white flowers during March and April.

Wild garlic what's what
★ The flowers and leaves are edible
★ Wild boar sometimes eat the bulbs
★ It often grows on the site of ancient woodlands
★ It has been used for centuries to make herbal medicines
★ Cats don't like it!

Harder to spot

WOW wildlife Otter

One of the Forest's most secretive animals, the otter is mainly active at night. A playful creature, it is an excellent swimmer and depends on unpolluted water and a good supply of fish.

How to recognise it
★ Long brown body and long tail
★ Lighter throat, whiskers
★ Webbed feet with claws

What it eats
Mainly fish, also frogs and birds occasionally

Four facts
1. Otters spend 3-5 hours a day hunting and can hold their breath for 4 mins in the water
2. They spend a lot of time out of water and bring up their young in a den called a holt, often found under roots or a rock.
3. They were once hunted for their coats which have dense fur for warmth
4. Signs of otters can sometimes be seen at Cannop Ponds, Soudley Brook and The River Lyd near Parkend

Slide
Otters sometimes leave a muddy slide where they slip into water

Otter cub on a muddy slide!

Be a detective

See if you can spot these two signs of otters around the Forest's rivers and ponds:

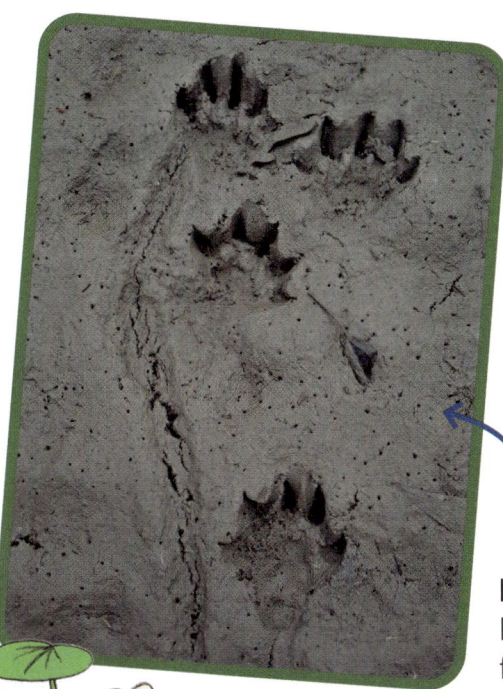

Footprints
Look in patches of mud or sand for tracks with five toes

Droppings
Otter poo is called spraint and can be seen on logs or rocks near water – it often contains fish bones

White-clawed crayfish

If you see what looks like a mini-lobster in one of the Forest's brooks then you may have been lucky enough to spot this rare crustacean, the UK's only native freshwater crayfish. Watch out you don't get nipped by its claws!

How to recognise it
★ Bronze coloured shell
★ Large claws are pale underneath

What it eats
Dead animals and plants, small water creatures, plants

Four facts
1. It was once common in the UK but is now rare due to water pollution and disease
2. It is found in shallow, clean streams, often under rocks
3. It is under threat from the invasive signal crayfish from North America which spreads a fatal 'plague' among native crayfish (there is now a scheme to protect white clawed crayfish by relocating them to safe rivers in Gloucestershire)
4. Like a crab its skeleton is on the outside

You can help protect native crayfish by staying out of waterways where there are warning signs about crayfish plague. Because they are protected you should also not pick up crayfish.

Interesting characters

Freshwater eel

If you are very lucky indeed, you might see a group of long dark shapes moving through one of the Forest's brooks, like black water snakes. These are eels, one of our most amazing and mysterious creatures.

How to recognise it
★ Long, snake-like body with no visible scales
★ Can be dark, silvery or olive green

What it eats
Dead animals, fish eggs, fish, insects and other invertebrates

Four facts
1. Eels can for live for up to 70 years
2. They can grow up to 1m long
3. They like brown, muddy water
4. Eels can slither over wet grass to reach places with deeper water

The remarkable life-cycle of the eel

Tides coming up the River Severn have brought eels to the Forest for thousands of years. Some swim up Blackpool Brook into the Forest but find their way blocked by a weir in Blakeney. In 2018 a special metal eel pass was built to help young eels wiggle up through a 'ladder' of bristles inside a metal case.

Blakeney eel pass

Eels need help!
In the past 40 years, numbers of freshwater eels in the UK have dropped by 95%. Pollution, climate change and over-fishing have been part of the cause. These migrating fish also find their routes blocked by dams, weirs, sluices and tidal barriers. Today eels are protected but also endangered.

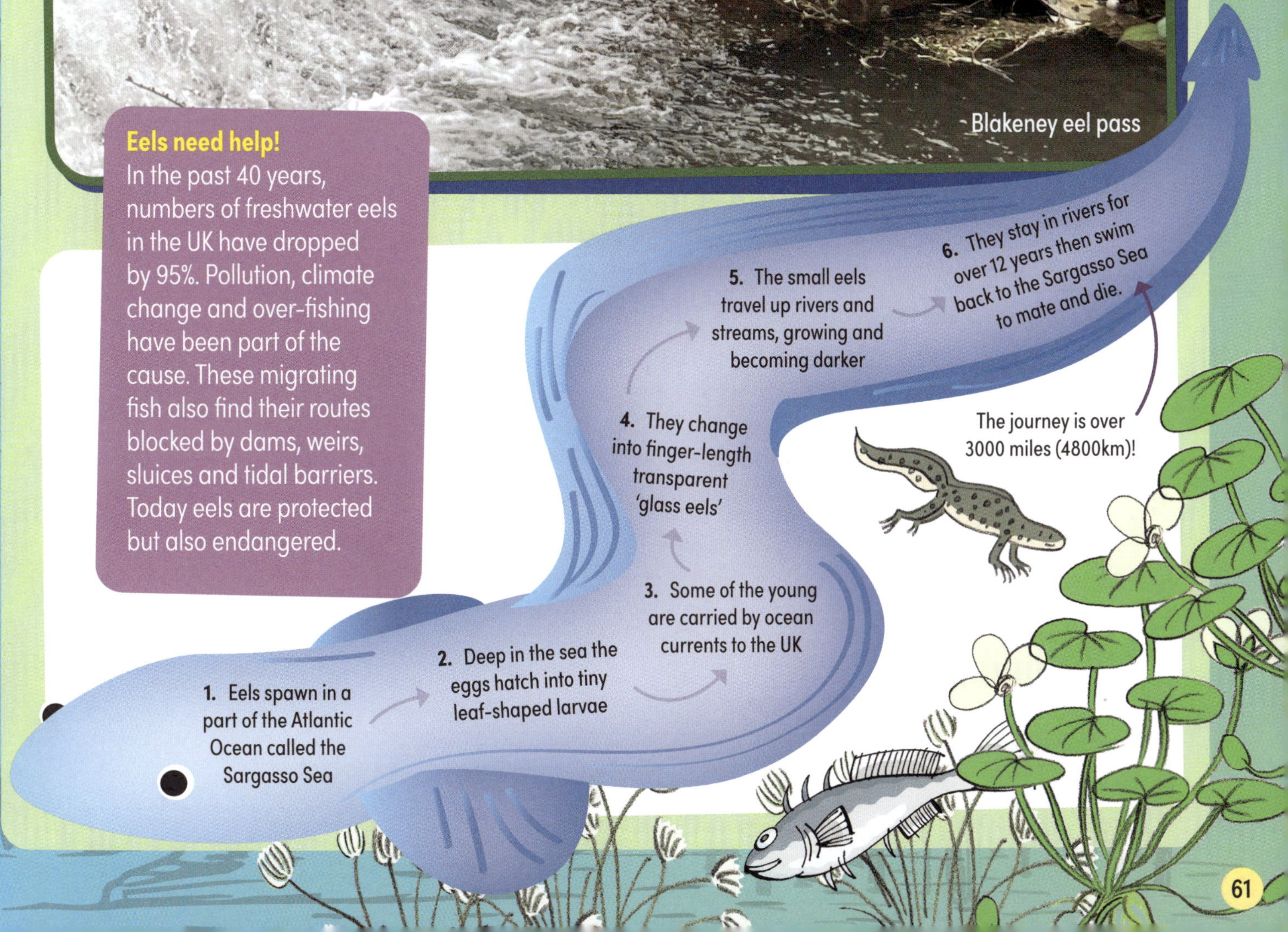

1. Eels spawn in a part of the Atlantic Ocean called the Sargasso Sea
2. Deep in the sea the eggs hatch into tiny leaf-shaped larvae
3. Some of the young are carried by ocean currents to the UK
4. They change into finger-length transparent 'glass eels'
5. The small eels travel up rivers and streams, growing and becoming darker
6. They stay in rivers for over 12 years then swim back to the Sargasso Sea to mate and die.

The journey is over 3000 miles (4800km)!

WOW wildlife: Beaver

Beavers are native to Britain and were once found across the Forest before being hunted to extinction for their fur, meat and body parts about 500 years ago. But now they are back, thanks to a special project where a pair of beavers from Scotland have been released into a purpose-built enclosure near Upper Lydbrook.

How to recognise it
★ Large and bulky with brown fur
★ Short legs and a big 'paddle' tail

What it eats
Bark and plants (they are fully vegetarian!)

Four facts
1. Beavers use their powerful teeth to fell small trees for food and to build dams
2. They use branches and mud to build a home called a lodge, with an underwater entrance
3. They dam shallow streams, like Greathough Brook in the Forest, to create deeper pools of water so they can swim safely to enter their lodge and find food.
4. The Forest's two beavers are kept in a large fenced enclosure so that they can build a wetland habitat in safety while being monitored carefully

Beavers: building and benefits
Removing trees lets in light which encourages plant growth and leads to richer habitats for wildlife

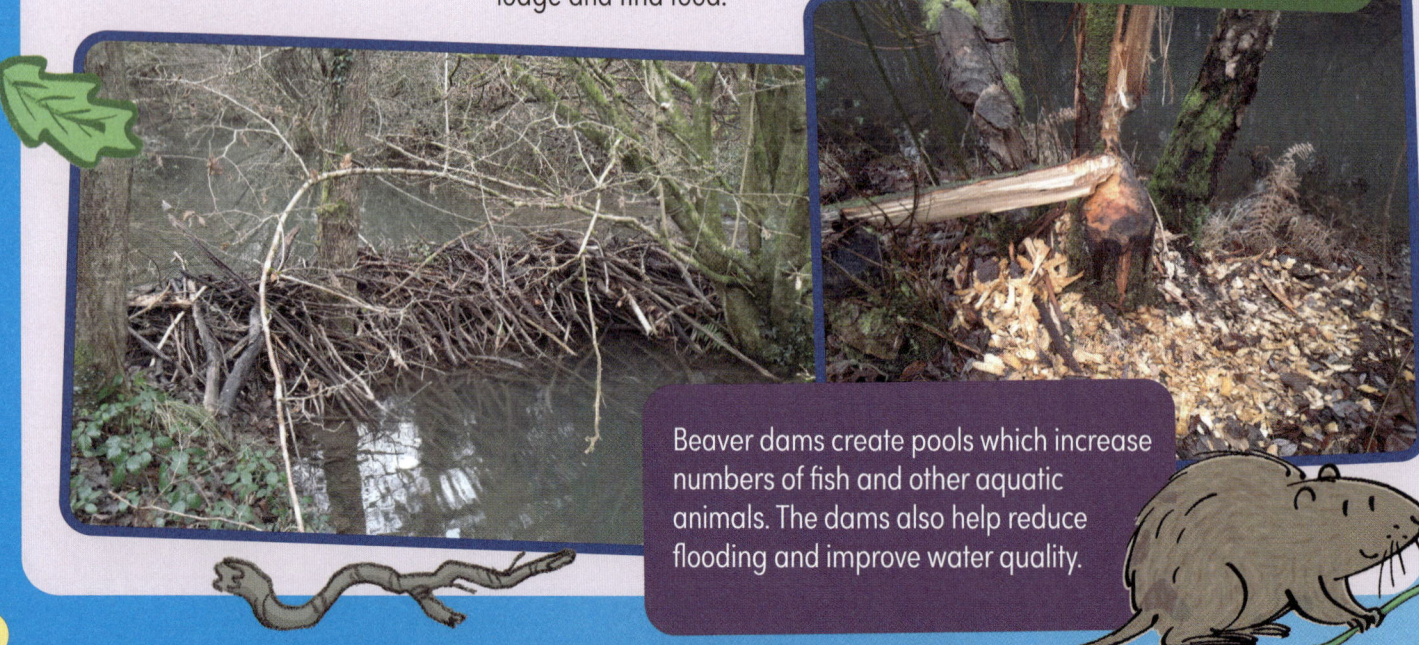

Beaver dams create pools which increase numbers of fish and other aquatic animals. The dams also help reduce flooding and improve water quality.

Bogs

Bogs might bring to your mind a picture of somewhere damp, dull or even stinky but, the reality is that they are special homes to all kinds of nature. Bogs form a mysterious, rich habitat that is halfway between land and water, and the Forest has a few of these spongy mini-wetlands.

Hobby

Large Red Damselfly

Smooth Newt

Bilberry

Cotton Grass

Foxes Bridge bog

Edgehills Bog, Mitcheldean

Edgehills Bog, Mitcheldean

Pondweed and sphagnum moss at Woorgreens

Look out for these

Smooth newt

These small amphibians are often well hidden in marshy grasslands where they hunt for any minibeasts they can fit in their mouths.

How to recognise it
★ Just 7-11cm long
★ Grey-brown with spotted orange belly
★ Males have a small crest in the breeding season

What it eats
Insects, larvae, worms and various small water creatures

Four facts
1. Newts are most active at night
2. Young newts leave the water in late summer when they lose their gills
3. They hibernate during the cold winter months
4. The smooth newt has the delightful scientific name Lissotriton vulgaris

Large red damselfly

With its thin, delicate body, this common insect can be seen around wet locations in late spring and summer.

How to recognise it
★ About 35mm long
★ Thin red and black body

What it eats
Small insects

Four facts
1. The female is mostly black
2. Like dragonflies, damselflies go through a nymph stage in water when they hatch
3. In spring the nymphs crawl out of the water after two years and transform into flying adults
4. They are easily harmed by water pollution

Harder to spot

Bilberry
On drier parts of boggy places and heathland you might be lucky enough to spot this low scrubby bush in late summer. It produces lots of small, dark berries which are like mini-blueberries and just as delicious.

Grass snake
Long, fast and harmless, the grass snake likes wetlands and is a good swimmer.

How to recognise it
★ Usually greenish with yellow marks near head
★ Small dark patches on its sides

What it eats
Frogs, toads, newts, fish and small mammals

Four facts
1. Prey is often still alive when swallowed whole
2. Grass snakes are often over 1m long
3. They can live for over 20 years
4. Females lay eggs in dark damp places (such as a garden compost heap), sometimes up to 30 at a time

Interesting characters

Hobby
A kestrel-sized falcon which can sometimes be spotted at Woorgreens chasing dragonflies across the lake at speed.

How to recognise it
★ Long pointed wings
★ Dark on top with lighter streaked plumage below

What it eats
Small birds such as swallows, insects

Four facts
1. The hobby is a fast and agile flier
2. It catches prey in flight and occasionally eats it on the wing
3. It has rusty brown feathers around its legs known as trousers
4. It uses old nests of other birds rather than making new ones

Bogs to visit
See the map on p6-7

Remember to take wellies as these places are always wet and muddy!

★ Edgehills Bog, near Cinderford
★ Foxes Bridge Bog, near Speech House
★ Woorgreens, near Speech House

Ponds and Pools

The Forest has lots of ponds and pools! One of the reasons for this is that there are lots of holes in the ground formed by mining and other industries. Over many years these can fill up with water and then attract plants and animals. Other pools of water have been specially built, like Cannop Ponds, which once supplied a waterwheel for an ironworks. Together, these bodies of water form a vital part of the Forest ecosystem.

Common Toad

Water Scorpion

Water Mint

Great Crested Newt

Leech

Mandarin Duck

Mallard's Pike Lake, Forest of Dean

A typical small Forest pond

Pond in Linear Park, Cinderford

Soudley Ponds

Look out for these

Mandarin duck

These spectacular water birds can be seen at Cannop Ponds and other sites around the Forest, although they are shy and like to stay under cover of trees.

How to recognise it
- ★ Males have red bill and bright plumage of different colours with extravagant feathers
- ★ Females are grey-brown with a mottled chest and blue markings

What it eats
Plants, seeds, snails and occasional small fish and frogs

Four facts
1. Another non-native animal, brought to the UK from China
2. Unlike most ducks, mandarins make their nests in trees!
3. Females lay 9-12 eggs in a hole, safe from predators like foxes
4. The young have to jump out of the nest when only 1-2 days old

Common toad

Toads spend most of the year looking for food or hibernating but in early spring they head to the Forest's ponds to breed.

How to recognise it
- ★ Olive-brown warty skin
- ★ Short legs
- ★ Walks rather than hops

What it eats
Slugs, snails, insects, worms

Four facts
1. Toads often hibernate through winter under log piles or rocks
2. They are less often eaten by predators than frogs because their skin contains foul-tasting toxins
3. Their tadpoles are toxic to fish too
4. Toads produce spawn in long strings which can be seen in ponds in spring

Broad-bodied chaser

This common dragonfly can be seen around ponds over summer. It's a very fast flyer with huge eyes.

How to recognise it
- ★ Male has plump blue body with yellow spots
- ★ Female is plump and brown

What it eats
Small insects such as gnats

Four facts
1. Chasers mate in mid-air
2. The female lays eggs in the water which hatch into larvae called nymphs
3. Males protect a territory and will fight off rivals
4. The broad-bodied chaser can fly backwards

Dragonflies dramas

The Forest is home to many types of dragonfly. These start life in ponds and rivers as nymphs, which often look a little like underwater beetles. These are greedy predators that prey on all kinds of small creatures using their special extending jaw.

Eventually, sometimes after 2-3 years, the nymph climbs out of the water on a plant to transform into an adult. Its body splits open and an adult dragonfly with wings emerges.

The acrobatic adults have flexible wings which allow them to hover and dart at up to 30mph. In addition their huge eyes enable them to spot prey such as mosquitoes and grab it in mid-air.

Good places to see dragonflies and smaller damselflies during the summer include Linear Park's ponds, Blackpool Brook, Woorgreens, Lightmoor Ponds and Soudley Ponds.

A dragonfly nymph

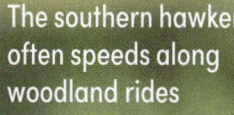

The southern hawker often speeds along woodland rides

Demoiselles flutter like butterflies and have amazing colours

Natty names
The UK's dragonflies include these:

★ Brilliant emerald
★ Ruddy darter
★ Dainty damselfly
★ Azure hawker
★ Beautiful demoiselle
★ Hairy dragonfly

Harder to spot

This amphibian is the UK's largest newt and a very exciting creature to see close at hand. Although it breeds in ponds it spends most of its life on land searching for food.

How to recognise it
★ Dark, warty skin with an orange belly and silver streak along the tail
★ Male has a large wavy crest along its back at breeding time
★ Looks like a mini-dinosaur!

What it eats
Any small creature such as insects, spiders, slugs as well as frogspawn and small newts

Four facts
1. Newts spend a lot of time on boggy grassland
2. They shelter under logs and stones
3. Predators include herons, ducks, magpies, snakes and large fish such as carp
4. They are protected by law and it is an offence to disturb newts or their eggs

Water scorpion

If you see something at the shallow edge of a pond that looks like a large beetle or a dead leaf then you may have discovered the fascinating water scorpion.

How to recognise it
★ Dark body, about 3.5cm long
★ Large pincer legs at front, thin tail at back

What it eats
Tadpoles, insect larvae and small fish

Four facts
1. These underwater predators are sometimes known as toe-biters
2. They are not real scorpions and cannot sting (and their nip is not painful) although they can fly
3. Once a victim is grabbed, its body is pierced and juices are sucked out
4. The water scorpion breathes through its bottom, using a snorkel-like tail!

Water mint

A plant that grows in and around ponds, water mint smells lovely, especially when the leaves are crushed. Look out for leaves which have been folded over in the water by a newt to protect the egg it has laid on them.

Interesting characters

Leech

Yes, there are bloodsucking worms to be found in ponds and rivers around the Forest! In fact there are lots of different types of leeches.

How to recognise it
★ Body often dark but can be greeny-brown also
★ Changes shape easily

What it eats
Blood from other pond animals

Four facts
1. Leeches have suckers on their head and rear end for piercing prey
2. They attach themselves to fish, tadpoles and snails to feed
3. Some types even feed on ducks, entering through the nostrils but not harming the host
4. Only one type (the medicinal leech) can consume human blood, and it is very rare.

Whirligig beetle

If you see some small shiny creatures whizzing around on a pond surface or a slow river then you've probably found whirligig beetles.

How to recognise it
★ 5-7mm long
★ Black, shiny and oval

What it eats
Small insects

Four facts
1. Its back legs are short and strong to act like paddles so it can speed about on the water looking for food
2. It can also dive underwater when hunting
3. Whirligig beetles have two sets of eyes: a pair to look up and another to see underwater!
4. Its name comes from the way it moves in circular patterns

Ponds and pools to visit

See the map on p6-7

Take care near water as it can be deep in places.

★ Crump Meadow, near Cinderford
★ Woorgreens, near Speech House
★ Linear Park/Ruspidge Halt, near Cinderford
★ Cannop Ponds, near Speech House
★ Wigpool, near Mitcheldean
★ Mallards Pike
★ Speech House Lake
★ Soudley Ponds

Forest Biodiversity Projects

Nine exciting community wildlife projects began in the Forest in 2017. These were part of the Foresters' Forest programme, funded by The National Lottery Heritage Fund, which aimed to help local people become more aware of the Forest and involved in caring for its many special habitats and features. Here are short summaries of the projects.

Ancient and notable trees

The Forest contains lots of old and special trees. This project aims to make people aware of these important trees and understand them and how to care for them.

What is an ancient tree?
- ★ An oak or yew over 300 years old
- ★ A beech or ash over 200 years old
- ★ A birch, cherry or hawthorn over 85-100 years old
- ★ A notable tree is special in some way or important to a local community

Why are ancient trees important?
Old trees tell a story and are often significant to local communities. They are also vitally important as wildlife habitats, supporting huge numbers of plants and animals, especially those such as insects and fungi which depend on dead and decaying wood.

Yew trees, like this one in Staunton, can live for over 1,000 years

The Culver Oak is one of the Forest's oldest

Some of the Forest's ancient and notable trees
- ★ The Old Man Oak
- ★ Forest Giant Oak
- ★ Verderer's Oak
- ★ Trafalgar Beech
- ★ Green Bottom Beech
- ★ Raven Cliff Lime
- ★ Speech House Hollies
- ★ Cockshoot Ash
- ★ Nailbridge Beech

Batscape

A greater horseshoe bat

The Forest of Dean and Wye Valley areas are especially important habitats for rare horseshoe bats.

In fact, one quarter of the UK's lesser horseshoe bats breed here (see page 48). The aim of the Batscape project is to better understand the Forest's bat roosting sites and feeding grounds and help to protect and improve them.

What is the 'batscape'?
Batscape refers to the places where bats sleep, breed, fly and feed. Different bats rely on different types of landscape: open spaces, hedgerows, woodlands and safe places where they can avoid being disturbed when at rest.

How people can help
★ Doing surveys of bat habitats
★ Counting bat numbers
★ Protecting roost sites and adding artificial ones
★ Planting hedges
★ Working with local landowners to improve bat-friendly habitats

Bat boxes

Birds

Because the Forest of Dean is made up of so many different kinds of habitats, it supports a huge range of birds. This project is all about improving and protecting these habitats and working with other projects to maintain the Forest's rich network of natural environments.

Priority species
This project has a special focus on five birds, which are in danger of declining in numbers:

★ Woodlark
★ Willow tit
★ Hawfinch
★ Nightjar
★ Tree pipit

The attractive willow tit is becoming increasingly rare

Helping the Forest's birds
RSPB experts are working with local volunteers to increase people's understanding of the needs of the Forest's key birds. Work also takes place to provide foraging and breeding habitats and to gather information about the number of birds in the area.

Butterflies

Around three-quarters of UK butterfly species are in decline and the Forest is now one of the last places where the endangered small pearl-bordered fritillary can be found. This project has been all about saving this species through providing the habitats it needs.

Lost habitats

Many of the Forest's butterflies have depended on woodland glades and clearings with grasslands. In recent decades, however, these important landscapes have been lost, partly due to increased tree cover and the spread of bracken etc, along with a decline in sheep grazing.

The small pearl-bordered fritillary caterpillar depends on violets for food

Small pearl-bordered fritillary adult

Volunteers planting violets on a newly made earth bank near Ruspidge Halt

Herdwick sheep

What the project has done
- ★ Gathered information about butterfly numbers and remaining habitats in the Forest
- ★ Conservation of existing butterfly habitats
- ★ Clearance of bracken and scrub to provide more grasslands suitable for the small pearl-bordered fritillary
- ★ Building earthworks and planting violets: the food plant for fritillary's larvae
- ★ Increasing the involvement and awareness of local people in the scheme
- ★ Introduced a grazing zone with tough Herdwick sheep to help maintain the open habitat

Conservation grazing

The Forest of Dean was once scattered with large numbers of grazing animals kept by miners, commoners and other local people: sheep, horses and cattle, mainly. These animals helped to maintain areas of open habitat which supported many animals, including butterflies, birds, reptiles and mammals. Grazing with livestock is now much reduced so this project has been all about bringing it back to the benefit of wildlife.

Highland cattle come to the Dean
Twelve hardy Highland cattle have been brought to nature reserves across the Forest to help restore important heathland. They roam freely, eating all kinds of plants and trampling bracken to help maintain a habitat which is good for invertebrates such as spiders and insects which feed birds. It also produces more grass for voles, which are prey for adders, and rough, damp areas for newts and other animals.

Nature reserves with conservation grazing
- ★ Woorgreens
- ★ Wigpool
- ★ Edgehills

Highland cattle at Woorgreens Nature Reserve

Exmoor ponies have also been used to preserve open habitats in the Forest

Woodland flora

This project is all about flowers and other plants. The Forest has many different types of plants because it sits on lots of types of rock which produce different types of soils. The woodland is also spread across hills, valleys, dry and wet areas, all providing habitats for a huge range of plants.

Aims of the project
1. To survey woodland plants across the Forest
2. To find the richest habitats in terms of ancient species
3. To preserve and improve these key areas
4. To increase native woodland in the long term

Woodland wildflowers
Here are just a few of the Forest's many interesting plants:

- ★ Stinking hellebore
- ★ Lesser periwinkle
- ★ Wood spurge
- ★ Garlic mustard
- ★ Yellow archangel
- ★ Lords and Ladies
- ★ Ragged robin
- ★ Enchanter's nightshade

Lords and ladies is a poisonous plant also called cuckoo pint

Dean's marvellous meadows

A wildflower meadow is a rich oasis of wildlife but sadly over 97% of these habitats have been lost across the UK in the past century. This project aims to protect and enhance the various small patches of wildflower meadow around the Forest in various ways.

Helping wildlife

Wildflower meadows are one of the key environments that link together the Forest's different habitats such as hedgerows, woods, streams, orchards, verges, ponds and paths. These joined up places allow animals to move around, find food, mate and thrive.

Lots of different plants = lots of different insects, such as this elephant hawk moth

Meadow help

The experts running this project have worked with local landowners, offering help with managing meadows:

★ Advice on topics such as cutting, grazing, controlling bracken
★ Small grants to help people manage their land in a sustainable way
★ Bringing meadow owners together to create a community of shared experience

A Forest meadow in flower

Waterways and ponds

The Forest of Dean has many small streams and over 200 ponds, plus many wet areas known as mires. These waterways provide important connections between the Forest's woodlands, open spaces, ponds, pools and bogs.

Crump Meadow Colliery Pond: a haven for wildlife

Aims of the project

1. To gather a team of volunteers to check over the Forest's many waterways
2. To find ways to improve and restore ponds
3. To develop many new ponds (two are currently being created in Milkwall and Ellwood)

River and pond life

The Waterways and Ponds project will help all kinds of wildlife to recover:

★ Fish
★ Amphibians
★ Reptiles
★ Birds
★ Invertebrates such as insects
★ Mosses and other plants

Reptiles

Sadly, reptiles are becoming rarer in most parts of the UK as their habitats come under threat from human activities such as farming and building. The Forest is an important location for reptiles and all four common species are found here. This project aims to help them continue to do well.

Forest reptiles
★ Adder
★ Common lizard
★ Slow worm
★ Grass snake

The grass snake is a quick-moving hunter

Reptiles expert David Dewsbury carrying out a survey

This project keeps track of numbers of reptiles across the Forest of Dean and educates people about the needs of these animals. The long-term aim is to make sure that there are plenty of habitats across the Forest which are favourable for reptiles and that these are protected.

Slow worm

Common lizard

79

People who look after nature in the Forest

Lots of different kinds of people help care for the Forest of Dean. Some of them have the important role of protecting its wildlife and helping it to it be flourishing and healthy. A big part of this involves making sure that habitats are well looked after, because living things depend on these. You can meet some of the people who do this special work here.

Name:	Leoni Dawson
Job title:	Community Ranger, Forestry England
What I do:	★ Work with volunteers (the Dean Green Team) who care for habitats to help wildlife to thrive. ★ Engage people in what we are doing in the Forest and why. ★ I complete walks, talks, events and activities to help people understand the wildlife of the Forest of Dean.

I really enjoy enthusing people and sparking interests, helping them nurture a lifelong love of where they live. Getting stuck in practically feels like I am doing some good for wildlife.

Name:	Kevin Caster
Job title:	Forest of Dean Nature Reserve Manager, Gloucestershire Wildlife Trust
What I do:	★ Manage habitats within the Forest of Dean for wildlife and people to enjoy. ★ Recreate and maintain wild spaces to help wildlife to thrive again and spread further across the Forest. ★ Protect the future for wildlife in a changing climate with increasing pressures on the landscapes all around.

After every winter's hard graft of habitat work follows a summer of rich wildlife gains that motivate me to do more each year.

Name:	Kate Wollen
Job title:	*Assistant Ecologist, Forestry England*
What I do:	★ Work on protecting the native wildlife of the Forest of Dean. ★ Try to expand the habitats available for so many of our species.

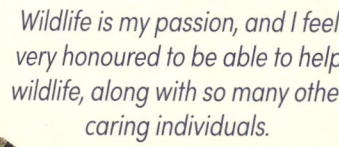

Wildlife is my passion, and I feel very honoured to be able to help wildlife, along with so many other caring individuals.

Name:	Emily Bennett
Job title:	*RSPB Assistant Warden / Assistant Conservation Officer*
What I do:	★ Survey and monitor birds and other species at Nagshead and Highnam Woods as well as across the Forest of Dean. ★ Carry out practical habitat management work to create a haven for the local wildlife.

I love my job because it allows me to spend time in nature and connect with the wildlife we have here. My role changes throughout the year and each new season brings a new set of exciting tasks to work on.

Name:	David Priddis
Job title:	*'Batman'*
What I do:	★ Amateur conservation, recording and research of bats, particularly horseshoe bats. ★ Help identify and protect roosts, Sites of Special Scientific Interest and bat habitat.

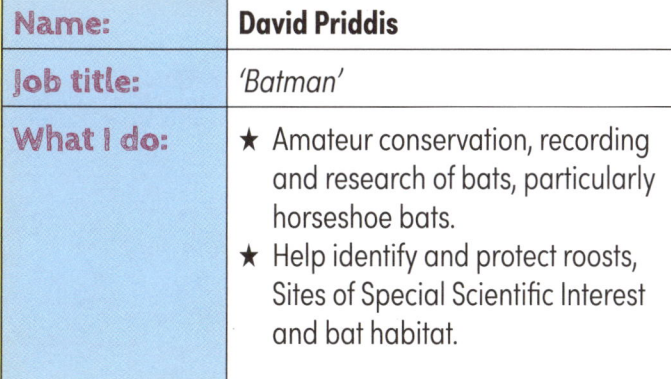

The more I learn about these flying mammals, the more amazing I realise they are.

81

Name:	**Rosie Kelsall**
Job title:	*Engagement Officer, Gloucestershire Wildlife Trust*
What I do:	★ Engage people with wildlife: adults, children, volunteers and local communities. ★ Help people to learn about, enjoy and understand the world around them.

I enjoy my job because every day I meet lots of people who want to learn more about out amazing wildlife, and I get a real buzz out of enthusing them.

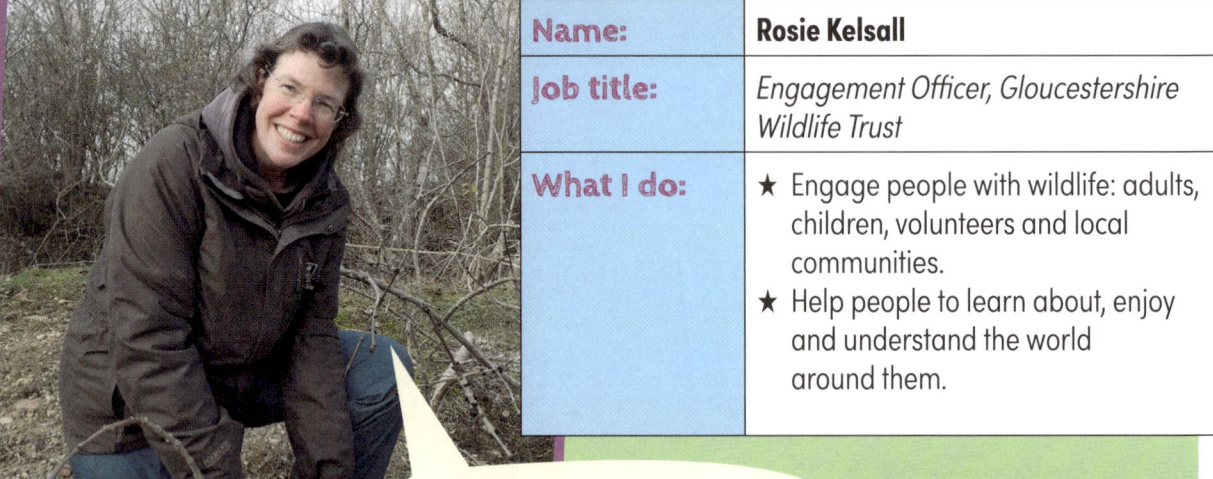

I enjoy what I do because I can do it for fun.

Name:	**David Dewsbury**
Job title:	*Amateur naturalist, Forest wildlife enthusiast and researcher*
What I do:	★ Carry out reptile and amphibian surveys and butterfly surveys. ★ Help Forestry England identify and maintain suitable places for these creatures to live.

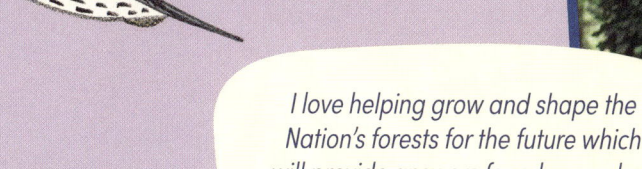

I love helping grow and shape the Nation's forests for the future which will provide answers for a low-carbon climate and biodiversity.

Name:	Ben Robinson
Job title:	Planning & Environment Manager, Forestry England
What I do:	★ Lead the Forestry England team in the Forest of Dean in charge of forest wildlife and habitats, and historic features. ★ long term planning to make sure the Forest flourishes.

Name:	Paul Rutter
Job title:	Leader for the Ancient and Notable Tree Project
What I do:	★ Find and record the locations of the oldest and remaining ancient trees in and around the Forest. ★ Record how these trees support a wide range of other species as they age including: plants, fungi, insects, birds and mammals, increasing the biodiversity of the Forest.

Spending time in and around ancient trees gives you a window into a rare historical landscape where wildlife still flourishes, and the trees make you feel good.

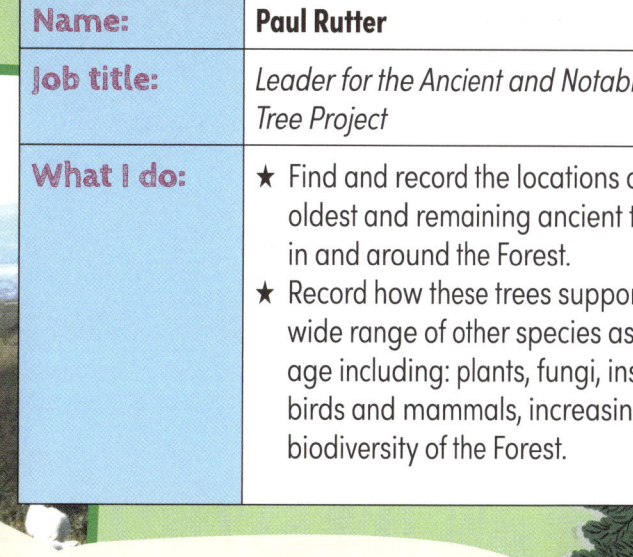

Native and non-native species

The wildlife of the Forest of Dean is a mix of animals and plants that have been here a very long time and others which have arrived more recently. This section will explain the difference between native and non-native species, and why this matters.

The weasel is a native mammal

Non-native species

Wildlife introduced to an ecosystem by human beings.

The pheasant is a non-native bird, brought to the UK from Asia

Native species

Living things that have become part of the Forest's ecosystem through the actions of nature.

Native and introduced (non-native) mammals

Here are some examples of Forest mammals for each group:

Native	Introduced
★ Mole	★ Rabbit
★ Hedgehog	★ Brown rat
★ Hazel dormouse	★ Grey squirrel
★ Red squirrel	★ American mink
★ Stoat	★ Fallow deer
★ Roe deer	

American mink

Invaders!

Invasive species are non-natives that have a damaging impact on other living things and environments. They can cause loss of native plants and animals, and harm sensitive habitats.

Some invasive animals in the Forest
- ★ **Grey squirrel** (they outcompete red squirrels and spread a harmful disease)
- ★ **Muntjac deer** (eat shrubs and woodland plants that other animals depend on)
- ★ **Signal crayfish** (carry a disease which kills native crayfish)
- ★ **Common carp** (a fish put into ponds which eats huge amounts of aquatic life)

Himalayan balsam, brought from Asia, has popping seeds which help spread the plant rapidly

Rhododendron flower

Some invasive plants in the Forest
- ★ **Himalayan balsam** (a very tall, quick-spreading flower that smothers riverbanks)
- ★ **Rhododendron** (a dense woody species that crowds out other plants and is toxic to some bees)
- ★ **Japanese knotweed** (spreads along streams, smothering plants, and can damage walls)
- ★ **Canadian pondweed** (grows quickly, often choking other pond life)

Controlling numbers
Sometimes both native and non-native animals have to be reduced in number in the Forest. This is done to prevent them causing too much damage to the ecosystem and harming important Forest operations such as growing new trees. Wild boar and deer numbers can both increase quickly, as they have no natural predators. Control of animals is done by trained Forest rangers.

Not everyone agrees that reducing numbers is a good way to deal with these problems: *What do you think?*

Damage to a sports pitch caused by boar searching for food

Sheep and grazing

Have you ever wondered why there are sheep roaming around parts of the Forest, including roads and villages? The sheep, along with other grazing animals, actually play an important part in preserving wildlife habitats across the area.

So, why sheep in a forest?
- For hundreds of years, the Dean was an important mining area, with lots of iron and coal pits.
- In medieval times Freeminers were often poor and so kept a few sheep loose around the woods to provide meat, wool, or money.
- This tradition (called commoning) grew over time, with some local people also letting their ponies and cattle wander round the Forest, grazing.
- Today, there are only a few 'sheep badgers' left and numbers of sheep are low after thousands were killed as a result of Foot and Mouth disease in 2001.

How does grazing livestock help wildlife?
1. Sheep eat lots of grass and plants, keeping open spaces from becoming overgrown.
2. They also trample quick-spreading plants like bracken.
3. Light grazing allows wildflowers to grow which are often food for insects.
4. The insects feed birds and amphibians which feed larger predators.

Herdwick sheep with local grazier Kate Batt, near Ruspidge Halt

The Birch Wood Green Project

A local shepherd, Kate Batt, has been keeping a group of Herdwick sheep in a fenced enclosure near Ruspidge Halt called Birch Wood Green. This is part of a special conservation project to help increase numbers of rare butterflies (see page 76) and other key species such as adders. The project includes three other grazing enclosures across the Forest.

The tree pipit is an example of a bird helped by sheep grazing

Sheep can be moved around to where they are needed

Why Herdwick sheep?
- They are a tough upland breed
- They will eat rough grass and plants that other sheep leave
- They can survive poor weather

How you can help
- Please don't feed the sheep!
- Keep dogs on leads
- Avoid disturbing the animals

Wildlife quizzes

Have a go at these woodland puzzles. Some of them are easy, some of them hard, and some can be worked out!

Trees

How well do you know the trees of the Forest?
See if you can identify each of these trees from their leaves and more. Answers on page 101.

Well-known trees

Trickier trees

Complex conifers

Barking up the wrong tree?

Now here is a tough challenge! Which trees are these? Answers on page 101.

1.
2.
3.
4.
5.

Fruits of the Forest

Do you know which trees these berries belong to? Answers on page 101.

1.
2.

Mixed up trees

Can you solve these woodland anagrams? Answers on page 101.

	Easy	Harder	Tough!
1.	has	charl	lared
2.	koa	dreel	northwah
3.	cheeb	noraw	carysome
4.	mile	cupers	spyscer
5.	wye	lazeh	thencuts

Forest challenge

Can you name...

1. 3 Forest birds beginning with S?
2. 4 Forest trees that are not conifers?
3. 3 Forest reptiles?
4. 2 Forest butterflies?
5. 5 woodland wildflowers?
6. 4 Forest animals that have red markings?
7. 1 Forest fungus?
8. 6 Forest animals beginning with B?

Answers on page 101.

Animal quiz

Mammals

Name the mammal. Answers on page 101.

Birds

Name the bird. Answers on page 101.

Plants Quiz

Name the plant. Answers on page 101.

Missing letter animals

What are these? They're all somewhere in this book! Answers on page 101.

Name	Clue
1. w _ _ _ b _ _ _	Snort snort!
2. t _ _ _ _ o _ _	Hoot hoot!
3. g _ _ _ _ _ _ _	Fast flyer
4. g _ _ _ w _ _ _	Bright at night
5. f _ _ _ _ _ d _ _ _ _	Big and spotty
6. g _ _ _ _ t _ _ _ _ b _ _ _ _ _	Scuttling hunter
7. g _ _ _ _ s _ _ _	Long and thin
8. s _ _ _ _ _ _ n _ _ _	Does wet and dry

The future of the Forest

The Forest of Dean is an important environment in so many ways. It is a rich mix of several different types of habitat, all blended together and connected. Unlike many other landscapes, it is also accessible for people to enjoy all year. But what does the future hold for the Forest?

An ever-changing place

Forests do not stand still. They are changing all the time and over the last 1,000 years, the Dean has seen a huge number of changes. At one point, in the 1600s, it had lost nearly all of its trees as they were cut down by people for fuel to make iron. The Forest we see today is the result of human activity still.

100 years ago several parts of the Forest looked like this!

It is important that people continue to shape the Forest now and in the future. If left completely alone, its precious open spaces would eventually be filled by trees. This habitat loss would lead to the loss of plants and animals and a poorer ecosystem. This section of the book sets out the various challenges that the Forest faces in the decades to come.

Challenges facing the Forest

1. Pests and diseases

Here are just some of the pests and diseases currently facing the wildlife of the Forest:

- **Ramorum disease** – this affects larches in particular but can also kill other trees including chestnuts
- **Ash dieback** – a fungal disease that attacks ash trees
- **Oak decline** – this could be a serious threat to the Dean's many oak woods
- **Pine weevils** – these insects harm young conifers and can destroy seedlings by feeding on their bark
- **Crayfish plague** (see page 60) – this may have already wiped out native crayfish in one of the Forest's brooks
- **Invasive species** (see page 84) – plants and animals which damage native species

A larch with ramorum disease

The large pine weevil

Forestry England and other organisations are working hard to counter these problems. For example, many larch and ash trees have been felled to try and prevent the further spread of diseases. Pests and invasive species are monitored and controlled where possible.

Loss of habitats

When Forest habitats are lost, especially open habitats, then the wildlife which depends on them will be lost too. Here's an example of what can happen, in this case if glades and grassy open spaces among the woodlands are not protected:

Scrub plants such as bracken and brambles quickly grow, smothering grasses and wildflowers.

Butterflies, bees and other insects which depend on these wildflowers die out, plus animals such as voles which eat plants.

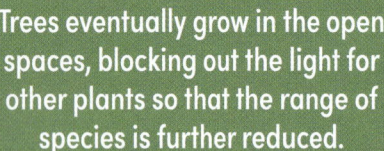

Birds which depend on insects for food are lost. Predators such as owls and foxes struggle to survive.

Trees eventually grow in the open spaces, blocking out the light for other plants so that the range of species is further reduced.

What can cause the loss of habitats?
★ A lack of sheep and other grazing animals
★ Uncontrolled spread of trees
★ Building developments
★ Poor management of land
★ Approaches to farming at the edges of the Forest which are not sensitive to the needs of wildlife, such as removing hedgerows.

An open space in woodland

Sheep and other grazers eat scrubby plants and tree seedlings

What is being done to stop habitat loss?
Forestry England, the organisation which manages the Forest of Dean, is very aware of these problems and is working with all kinds of groups and local communities to help protect and conserve the Forest's many different habitats. The many biodiversity projects featured on pages 74-79 are examples of what is being done to help prevent the decline in species.

Plans are also in place so that ongoing forestry work is beneficial to wildlife as far as possible, for example by planting the right tree in the right place for various environments.

3. Making sure habitats are connected

Animals, like human beings, do not stay in one place – they need to move around to thrive. This is especially important as changes happen to the Forest over time, such as those caused by global warming. Where habitats are isolated or in small fragments that are not connected, wildlife cannot easily move around to find food, shelter or a mate to reproduce.

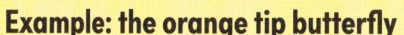

A female orange tip feeding on nectar

Example: the orange tip butterfly
★ The orange tip needs open spaces where the flowers grow which it feeds on
★ It needs to be able to move around to attract a mate
★ After mating the female needs to find cuckooflower plants to lay her eggs on
★ The caterpillars eat the cuckooflower and develop into adult butterflies

A butterfly in an isolated meadow in the Forest surrounded by dense woodland or busy roads or buildings could struggle to find food, locate a mate or find plants to lay eggs on.

Similar situations happen to other insects and to birds, mammals, reptiles and more.

How can Forest habitats be joined up?
★ One answer is to make habitats larger so they can accommodate more species. We can also make sure that habitats are well suited to the animals that live in them.
★ New areas of habitat can also be created, to allow easier movement of species.
★ Strips of 'joining' land can also be carefully managed to encourage wildlife to access new areas – these include paths, tracks, roadside verges, gardens, riverbanks, hedges, orchards and churchyards.

The Recreation Ground at Pillowell is an example of a valuable meadow habitat that has recently been restored and protected by keen local volunteers.

4. Managing visitors to the Forest

The Forest of Dean is visited by thousands of people each month. It is popular both with locals and people who travel here to enjoy the area's attractions, walk through the woods or take part in activities such as cycling, running, canoeing or climbing. Most visitors are sensitive to the needs of nature, but problems do sometimes occur:

★ Litter
★ Fires
★ Dogs disturbing sheep and other animals such as ground nesting birds
★ People making new mountain bike trails without permission

Fly tipping is illegal and can be very harmful to wildlife

The people who manage the Forest work hard to maintain good facilities for visitors and allow people to access the area freely, but sometimes fences need to be put up to protect special areas of new planting or for conservation grazing and other projects. Local people are often involved in these projects, and information boards are sometimes put up to explain what is going on. The future of the Forest depends on balancing the needs of timber production, visitors and wildlife.

A sustainable Forest

We need wood from trees for all kind of things including building houses and making furniture. Is it better that this timber comes from well managed UK forests or is it better to import it from other countries where it may not be produced in a sustainable way? A sustainable forest means one which can be maintained over time without serious environmental damage.

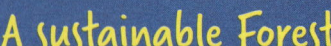

When walking in the woods people may come across harvesting operations and machines like this, showing that the Forest is a working landscape as well as an ecosystem. The trees are grown as a crop, and felling them provides important timber for the country, supplies incomes to support Forestry England's work and creates jobs for local contractors.

5. Protecting valuable features

One of the Forest's old beech trees

The Forest is home to some large, old trees, as described on page 74 (Ancient and Notable Trees project). Many of these are mature oak and beech trees, over 200 years old. These trees support a huge range of living things from animals and plants to fungi and lichens. Many of them have dead and fallen branches with decaying wood. This rotting material plays a really important part in feeding all kinds of organisms which then act as food for others.

Without protection and conservation these trees can be lost. They can be overshadowed by taller conifers blocking out the light they depend on to make food, for example. Or they can suffer from stress due to the soil being waterlogged or dried out as climate change causes extreme weather conditions. They can also be damaged by human activity.

Fortunately, the Forest has a number of nature reserves and specially protected sites, but the most important features and places will need careful protection and monitoring if they are to be there for generations to come.

6. Keeping track of significant animals

Deer eating bark

As this book describes, the Forest is home to hundreds of amazing animals of all kinds. Three mammals have a particularly big impact on the Forest's ecosystem: boar, deer and squirrels. This is partly because the numbers of these animals can increase quickly. In 2008, for example, there were fewer than 150 wild boar in the woodlands but by 2018 this had increased to an estimated 1,600.

Grey squirrels and deer can both cause considerable damage to trees if their numbers become too high. In the long term this can have a negative effect on the Forest's habitats. Because of this, it is vital to keep track of these animals and study the impact that they have on the Forest so that the right action can be taken to benefit the whole ecosystem.

Climate change

The biggest threat to the Forest in the long term may be the change in our climate caused by global warming. Climate change is leading to more extremes of weather such as droughts, storms and floods. Milder winters also means that fewer pests are killed off by hard frosts.

Some ways in which climate change could affect the Forest
- Periods of very hot/dry and very wet weather can stress and eventually kill some of the Forest's key trees, including oaks
- Warmer weather could see a further increase in diseases which affect trees
- Temperature rises will change the kinds of plants that grow in the area – this will change the insects and could lead to the loss of some types of birds, for example
- Bogs and mires could dry out in summer droughts, leading to wetland species dying out
- Some meadow flowers which rely on damp conditions could be lost
- River wildlife could be damaged by heavy rainfall causing floods which wash away their homes

The loss of trees could be especially damaging as trees play a very important role in storing carbon, one of the substances which is behind global warming. Trees also produce oxygen, which living things need to breathe.

What can be done?
Forestry England is finding out if new species of trees can be grown in the Forest which can survive extremes of weather. It is also sourcing seeds for planting trees, such as oak, from places with warmer climates, such as Southern Europe. It is difficult to know how the Forest's native plants and animals can be protected from climate change, however. Wildlife experts are monitoring species to see how they are being affected and to find out if they can adapt and survive.

Tree planting

Reducing floods
Some action is being taken to counter the effects of climate change. Steps have already been taken to reduce floods in and around the Forest, such as the one which badly affected Lydbrook in 2019.

- Larger wetland areas are being created to store water in the ground
- Barriers of branches (brash) have been put in place to slow down rainwater as it drains into brooks
- Woody waste material is put into streams to slow down the flow of water
- Beavers have been brought in to make dams and pools which also help control floodwater (see page 62).

One of the beaver dams in the Forest

Our Shared Forest

A plan for the future of the Forest of Dean has been put together called 'Our Shared Forest'. This plan will shape the Forest over the next 100 years and provide guidance for the management of wildlife and wild spaces. The plans include the following aims:

★ To make sure Forest habitats are large enough so that nature itself can take care of them
★ For habitats to be connected, so species can benefit from moving around
★ For wetlands and waterways to thrive
★ To maintain open spaces with grazing animals
★ To ensure a diverse mix of woodlands including young and old trees
★ To bring back lost native animals and plants where possible

Could the native red squirrel return to the Forest one day?

By protecting and managing a diverse mix of woodlands, and bringing back more native wildlife such as beavers, the Forest will continue to thrive for us all to enjoy.

97

Projects you can join

The best way to find out more about the wildlife of the Forest of Dean is to get close to it! There are various groups, projects and events that families and children can become part of. Going along to these gives you an opportunity to meet experts, learn new things and become actively involved in caring for the wild animals, plants and their habitats. It's fun too!

Counting newts

Birds

RSPB (Royal Society for the Protection of Birds)
The RSPB has nature reserves at Nagshead and Highnam Woods. They run events for children during the summer, advertised on their websites:

Visit www.rspb.org.uk/reserves-and-events/reserves-a-z/nagshead/ and www.rspb.org.uk/reserves-and-events/reserves-a-z/highnam-woods/

Email **Nagshead@rspb.org.uk** or **Highnam.woods@rspb.org.uk**

Ponds and reptiles

Newt and reptile surveys with David Dewsbury

Email **westengland@forestryengland.uk**

Bats

Gloucestershire Wildlife Trust and Gloucestershire Bat Group hold events for people who are interested.

Gloucestershire Bat Group
glosbats.org.uk

Bat Conservation Trust
www.bats.org.uk

Grazing animals

Ponies and Highland cattle
Gloucestershire Wildlife Trust welcomes volunteers to help with practical winter tasks, summer surveys or year-round grazing animal welfare checks.

Email **info@gloucestershirewildlifetrust.co.uk**

GWT groups for children and families

Gloucestershire Wildlife Trust
GWT Nature tots: For pre-school aged children, meets once a month in Coleford.
www.gloucestershirewildlifetrust.co.uk

Forest Explorers: For family groups, meets once a month at weekends, explores different aspects of forest nature.
Email **forestexplorersfod@gmail.com**

For older children

Wye Valley AONB Youth Rangers
Youth Rangers: For teenagers (14-18) to attend on their own, to explore all sorts of heritage, run by Wye Valley AONB.

Visit **www.wyevalleyaonb.org.uk/caring-for-wye-valley-aonb/youth-rangers/**

Email **community@wyevalleyaonb.org.uk**

For families

The Rewild Project
This project's aim is to re-connect people to nature and heritage through arts and crafts, growing food, outdoor learning and community-building projects in the Forest of Dean.
www.therewildproject.com

Community projects

Pillowell Recreation Ground
A group of volunteers doing excellent work with wildlife and habitats. The group runs a Facebook page with updates (search on Facebook)
Email **pillowellrec.info@btinternet.com**

Friends of Worcester Walk
This is another very active group which has been supported by Foresters' Forest. The group runs a Facebook page with updates (search on Facebook)

Time to throw in a newt trap! Part of a pond survey in 2021

To find out more about Forest wildlife:

★ Use the books in your local library – they are free to borrow!
★ Look at the Gloucestershire Wildlife Trust website:
www.gloucestershirewildlifetrust.co.uk

To volunteer on projects in the Forest of Dean, contact Forest Voluntary Action Forum, email: **volunteer@fvaf.org**

Answers

Page 22: Beech woods – Be a detective
A. A small mammal, probably a rabbit
B. Beetle larvae
C. A woodpecker
D. A fox (an old unused burrow)
E. A vole or other small rodent

Page 25: Know your cones
From left to right:
Pine, fir, spruce, larch

Page 30: Conifer woods – What is that?
A. Earthball fungus
This looks like a warty potato and often grows near paths. It is a toxic fungus, not to be confused with the much whiter puffball.

B. Woodpigeon eggshell
Large white eggs often belong to birds in the dove family, and the woodpigeon is the largest.

C. Tree resin
Resin is a sticky goo that trees make to deal with pests or damage. It sets hard to seal wounds. It is seen more often on conifers, such as this larch tree.

Page 16: Oak Woods – What is that?
A. knopper gall
This is a strange growth found on oak trees. It is caused by a tiny wasp which lays its eggs on a developing acorn. The larva releases chemicals which cause the oak tree to make a wobbly growth around the larva. This protects it as it feeds inside. It does not damage the tree.

B. Mazegill fungus
This is a toxic fungus that grows on oaks. It can damage trees by causing a disease called brown rot.

C. Wasp galls
These common shapes on oak leaves are caused by very small wasps laying their eggs on the leaf. Inside each gall is a wasp larva feeding on the leaf. These are spangle galls (top) and silk button galls (below).

Page 51: Be a detective – What has eaten what?
A. A bird (probably a pigeon) has been eaten by bird of prey or a fox
B. This fungus has been nibbled by a rodent such as a mouse
C. A fir cone, broken apart by a squirrel for its seeds
D. Hazelnut shells with the nuts inside eaten by mice
E. Tree bark stripped by deer

Page 51: Rides, paths and edges – What is that?
A. Vapourer moth caterpillar
This is a really striking larva which can sometimes be seen on oaks where it feeds. As with many other hairy caterpillars, touching it can cause irritation so beware.

B. Egg of the white letter hairstreak butterfly
This UFO-like egg is very small and very rare. The butterfly is rarely spotted in the Forest because its larvae depend on elm trees which are not common locally.

C. Ivy stem
Many of the Forest's trees are covered in ivy, a climbing plant which uses trunks and branches to support itself. Ivy sends out small root hairs which glue onto surfaces such as bark. It does not damage trees and it also acts as a shelter to animals.

Page 55: Mining spoil heaps and quarries – What is that?
A. Yellow brain fungus
If you see a bright orange jelly-like splodge on a dead branch then it is probably yellow brain fungus, which feeds on other fungi. It is the subject of many myths and was once said to be the sign of a witch's spell.

B. Bird pellet
You may have heard of owl pellets but many of the Forest's larger birds, such as buzzards, sparrowhawks and crows cough up hairy balls of small bones, seeds, fur, teeth and more – the parts of prey or a meal which cannot be digested.

C. Hair ice
This rare and beautiful winter phenomenon is found in damp places where there is rotting wood and the air has dropped to freezing point. It can sometimes be seen on the old railway track between Whitecroft and Moseley Green.

Pages 87-88: Trees quiz
Well-known trees
1. Sycamore
2. Beech
3. Oak
4. Sweet chestnut
5. Holly

Trickier trees
1. Ash
2. Alder
3. Silver birch
4. Rowan (mountain ash)
5. Hawthorn

Complex conifers
1. Scots pine
2. Norway spruce
3. Larch

Barking up the wrong tree?
1. Beech
2. Sweet chestnut
3. Oak
4. Scots pine
5. Silver birch

Fruits of the Forest
1. Hawthorn
2. Rowan (mountain ash)

Page 88: Mixed up trees

	Easy	Harder	Tough!
1.	ash	larch	alder
2.	oak	elder	hawthorn
3.	beech	rowan	sycamore
4.	lime	spruce	cypress
5.	yew	hazel	chestnut

Page 88: Forest challenge
Examples of possible correct answers:
1. Song thrush, swan, starling, sparrowhawk, stonechat, spotted flycatcher, siskin
2. Oak, beech, sweet chestnut, holly, ash, hawthorn, willow, rowan
3. Adder, grass snake, lizard, slow worm
4. Large white, small white, common blue, orange tip, brimstone, grizzled skipper, small pearl-bordered fritillary, purple hairstreak
5. Bluebell, wild garlic, foxglove, honeysuckle, buttercup, herb Robert, purple orchid, bird's foot trefoil, buddleia, Himalayan balsam
6. Ladybird, great spotted woodpecker, cinnabar moth, robin, cardinal beetle, stonechat, red damselfly, vapourer moth larva, pheasant, mandarin duck, red admiral
7. Turkey tail fungus, beefsteak fungus, chicken of the woods, fly agaric, scarlet elf cup, stinkhorn, earthball, yellow brain fungus
8. Badger, bat, beaver, boar, brown rat, blackbird, blue tit, buzzard, barn owl, bullfinch, bee, beetle, butterfly, brilliant emerald dragonfly, brown trout

Page 89: Animals quiz
Mammals
1. Common vole
2. Stoat
3. Common shrew

Birds
1. Goldcrest
2. Grey heron
3. Song thrush

Page 89: Plants Quiz
1. Old man's beard (traveller's joy)
2. Bramble (blackberry)
3. Wood anemone

Page 89: Missing letter animals
1. Wild boar
2. Tawny owl
3. Goshawk
4. Glow worm
5. Fallow deer
6. Green tiger beetle
7. Grass snake
8. Smooth newt

Image credits

Pine marten

Nuthatch

Page 1: fallow buck, Forestry England; **Page 2:** common blue butterfly, David Dewsbury; **Page 4:** Forest in spring, tom c licensed with CC BY-SA 2.0.; **Page 4:** Foxes Bridge Colliery, Dean Heritage Centre; **Page 4:** Forest path, Forestry England; **Page 5:** meadow, Chris Parsons; **Page 5:** pine marten, Mark Hamblin 2020VISION; **Page 5:** fallow buck, Ray Buckley; **Page 6:** map, Kate Sheppard; **Page 9:** Shaden Tuft Oak, Sue Middleton; **Page 10:** great spotted woodpecker, David Priddis; **Page 10:** nuthatch, David Priddis; **Page 10:** treecreeper, David Priddis; **Page 11:** bluebells, David Priddis; **Page 11:** herb Robert, Julie (thanks for 10 million views) licensed with CC BY-NC-SA 2.0.; **Page 11:** oak moss, Andy Seed; **Page 12:** boar with young, Kristian Bell/Shutterstock.com; **Page 12:** male boar, Eric Isselee/Shutterstock.com; **Page 12:** boar jaw, Andy Seed; **Page 13:** rooting boar, Erni/Shutterstock.com; **Page 13:** 5 'Be a detective' images, Andy Seed; **Page 14:** redstart, tsbl2000 licensed with CC BY-ND 2.0.; **Page 14:** fallow deer, Forestry Commission Isobel Cameron; **Page 14:** roe deer, Forestry Commission; **Page 15:** spotted longhorn beetle, David Dewsbury; **Page 15:** silver washed fritillary, David Dewsbury; **Page 15:** chicken of the woods, rodtuk licensed with CC BY-NC-SA.; **Page 16:** jay, Piotr Krzeslak/Sutterstock.com; **Page 16:** woodcock, Forestry Commission Douglas Green; **Page 16:** pied flycatcher, Erni/Shutterstock.com; **Page 16:** 3 'what is that?' images, Andy Seed; **Page 17:** 2 oak woods images, Sue Middleton; **Page 19:** beeches in autumn, Andy Seed; **Page 20:** grey squirrel, Forestry Commission; **Page 20:** damaged tree, Andy Seed; **Page 20:** dor beetle, Forestry Commission; **Page 20:** lichen, Andy Seed; **Page 21:** tawny owl, Forestry Commission; **Page 21:** wood warbler, Erni/Shutterstock.com; **Page 21:** turkey tail fungus, Holly Pretious; **Page 21:** bird's nest orchid, PJ Photography/Shutterstock.com; **Page 22:** woodpecker hole in tree, Paul Rutter; **Page 22:** 4 burrow images, Andy Seed; **Page 22:** hawfinch, David Priddis; **Page 23:** hazel catkins, swallowtail; **Page 23:** coppiced hazel, Dominic's pics licensed with CC BY 2.0.; **Page 23:** hazel dormouse, Stuart Sutton; **Page 25:** conifer illustrations, Irina Simkina/Shutterstock.com, lubbas/Shutterstock.com, nikiteev_konstantin/Shutterstock.com; **Page 25:** cones, Andy Seed; **Page 26:** siskin, susie2778 licensed with CC BY-NC 2.0.; **Page 26:** walnut orb spider, AlexandreRoux01 licensed with CC BY-NC-SA 2.0.; **Page 26:** foxgloves, Helen Chick; **Page 26:** beard lichen, loarie licensed with CC BY 2.0.; **Page 27:** goshawk, iStock.com/Nature Photography; **Page 27:** firecrest, Michal Pesata/Shutterstock.com; **Page 28:** crossbill, Michalicenko/Shutterstock.com; **Page 28:** wood ant, Forestry Commission; **Page 28:** wood ant nest, Sue Middleton; **Page 29:** pine marten in grass, Mark Hamblin 2020VISION **Page 29:** pine marten climbing tree, Joop Beermann/Shutterstock.com; **Page 30:** muntjac, Forestry Commission; **Page 30:** 3 'What is that?' images, Andy Seed; **Page 31:** deer prints, Weldon Schloneger/Shutterstock.com; **Page 31:** 4 'Be a Detective' images, Andy Seed; **Page 33:** meadow, Chris Parsons; **Page 33:** buzzard, David Priddis; **Page 34:** cinnabar, nutmeg66 licensed with CC BY-NC-ND 2.0.; **Page 34:** large white butterfly, Forestry Commission; **Page 34:** meadow grasshopper, Allan Hopkins licensed with CC BY-NC-ND 2.0.; **Page 35:** orchids and meadow flowers, Sue Middleton; **Page 35:** adder's tongue, Kentish Plumber licensed with CC BY-NC-ND 2.0.; **Page 35:** dung beetles, Andy Seed; **Page 35:** quaking grass, Durlston Country Park licensed with CC BY-NC-SA 2.0.; **Page 36:** barn owl, NCaan/Shutterstock.com; **Page 36:** small pearl-bordered fritillary, David Dewsbury; **Page 36:** waxcap fungi, Forestry Commission Isobel Cameron; **Page 37:** Mother Shipton moth, Alistair Hobbs is licensed with CC BY-NC-SA 2.0.; **Page 39:** Worgreens with foxgloves, Martin Fowler/Alamy Stock Photo; **Page 39:** Woorgreens in autumn, Andy Seed; **Page 40:** Common blue butterfly, David Dewsbury; **Page 40:** stonechat, Jo Reeve licensed with CC BY 2.0.; **Page 40:** common lizard, David Elder; **Page 41:** golden-ringed dragonfly on tree, Paul:Ritchie licensed with CC BY-NC-ND 2.0.; **Page 41:** golden-ringed dragonfly on heather, Nick Greaves/Shutterstock.com; **Page 41:** birds-foot trefoil, Vertigogen licensed with CC BY-NC-SA 2.0.; **Page 42:** adder in bracken, David Dewsbury; **Page 42:** small adder, iStock.com/MikeLane45; **Page 42:** palmate newt, Erni/Shutterstock.com; **Page 42:** palmate newts swimming, Rudmer Zwerver/Shutterstock.com; **Page 43:** nightjar on ground, Ian Brownlee **Page 43:** nightjar with open mouth, WildlifeWorld/Shutterstock.com; **Page 43:** green tiger beetle, David Dewsbury **Page 45:** woodland ride, Forestry England **Page 45:** Autumn in the Forest, Greens and Blues/Shutterstock.com; **Page 45:** Speckled Wood Butterfly, Stephan Morris/Shutterstock.com; **Page 46:** Fox, Giedriius/Shutterstock.com; **Page 46:** brimstone butterfly, naturalengland licensed with CC BY-NC-ND 2.0.; **Page 46:** long-tailed tit, David Priddis; **Page 47:** orange tip butterfly, jeannie debs licensed with CC BY 2.0.; **Page 47:** buff-tailed bumblebee, Aardwolf6886 licensed with CC BY-ND 2.0.; **Page 47:** bracken, Andy Seed; **Page 47:** honeysuckle flower, Sally Payne is licensed with CC BY-NC-ND 2.0.; **Page 47:** honeysuckle stems, Andy Seed; **Page 48:** lesser horseshoe bats, David Priddis; **Page 48:** bat in flight, Rudmer Zwerver/Shutterstock.com; **Page 49:** Greater horseshow bat, francesco de marco/Shutterstock.com; **Page 49:** thermometer, jkcDesign/Shutterstock.com; **Page 49:** oak leaf, red ladybird, Lana_Samcorp/Shutterstock.com; **Page 49:** brown long-eared bat, COULANGES/Shutterstock.com; **Page 49:** noctule bat, Mnolf licensed with CC BY-SA 3.0.; **Page 49:** red-headed cardinal beetle, David Dewsbury; **Page 49:** fly agaric, Barbara Seed; **Page 50:** glow worm at night, David Dewsbury; **Page 50:** glow worm in daylight, Eric Isselee/Shutterstock.com; **Page 50:** wasp beetle on rock, David Dewsbury; **Page 50:** wasp beetle from side, AGAMI Photo Agency/Alamy Stock Photo; **Page 51:** 5 images for 'Be a detective', Andy Seed **Page 51:** larva, nature: close-up & colourful licensed with CC BY-NC-ND 2.0.; **Page 51:** White-letter Hairstreak butterfly ovum, Tony Moore;

Waxcap funghi

Glow worm

Page 51: ivy, Andy Seed; **Page 53:** quarry, Andy Seed; **Page 53:** ravens, Krasula/Shutterstock.com; **Page 54:** slow worm, David Dewsbury; **Page 54:** spleenwort, Philip_Goddard licensed with CC BY-NC 2.0.; **Page 54:** peregrine falcon, Sririam Bird Photographer/Shutterstock.com; **Page 54:** buddleia, Marcwiegelmann/Shutterstock.com **Page 55:** crab spider, David Dewsbury; **Page 55:** grizzled skipper, David Dewsbury; **Page 55:** yellow brain fungus, Andy Seed; **Page 55:** owl pellet, far closer licensed with CC BY 2.0.; **Page 55:** hair ice, Andy Seed; **Page 57:** Blackpool Brook, Andy Seed **Page 57:** kingfisher, Forestry Commission; **Page 58:** dipper, Ihor Hvozdetskyi/Shutterstock.com; **Page 58:** green shield bug, Darius Baužys licensed with CC BY-SA 2.0.; **Page 58:** wild garlic, Rupert Barry; **Page 59:** otter on log, Bildagentur Zoonar GmbH/Shutterstock.com; **Page 59:** otter footprints, Lukaspich/Shutterstock.com; **Page 59:** otter droppings, iStock.com/Cloebudgie; **Page 60:** crayfish, Linda Pitkin 2020VISION; **Page 60:** eel, Rostislav Stefanek/Shutterstock.com; **Page 60:** eel vector, Nadzin/Shutterstock.com; **Page 61:** Blakeney eel pass, Sue Middleton; **Page 62:** beaver, Kate Wollen Forestry England; **Page 62:** beaver dam, Andy Seed; **Page 62:** beaver tree felling, Andy Seed; **Page 63:** Biblins Bridge, Sue Middleton; **Page 63:** Forest brook, Ellie Matsanova/Shutterstock.com; **Page 63:** heron illustration, Caterina_K/Shutterstock.com; **Page 63:** trout illustration, ankomando/Shutterstock.com; **Page 63:** mayfly illustration, H.Elvin/Shutterstock.com; **Page 63:** shrimp illustration, MarySan/Shutterstock.com; **Page 63:** algae illustration, Toltemara/Shutterstock.com; **Page 65:** Foxes Bridge bog, Sue Middleton; **Page 65:** Edgehills bog, David Broadbent/Alamy Stock Photo; **Page 65:** Edgehills bog, David Broadbent/Alamy Stock Photo; **Page 65:** moss and pondweed, Nature Picture Library/Alamy Stock Photo; **Page 66:** smooth newt, Petr Muckstein/Shutterstock.com; **Page 66:** large red damselfly, David Priddis; **Page 67:** grass snake, Stephan Morris/Shutterstock.com; **Page 67:** bilberries, Nata Naumovec/Shutterstock.com; **Page 67:** hobby, Dennis Jacobsen/Shutterstock.com; **Page 69:** Mallards Pike, iStock.com/russellbinns; **Page 69:** small Forest pond, Andy Seed **Page 69:** Linear Park, Martin Fowler/Alamy Stock Photo; **Page 69:** Soudley Ponds, A ROOM WITH VIEWS/Alamy Stock Photo; **Page 70:** Mandarin ducks, GG6369/Shutterstock.com; **Page 70:** common toad, David Priddis; **Page 70:** broad-bodied chaser, David Priddis; **Page 71:** dragonfly nymph, David Priddis; **Page 71:** southern hawker, nutmeg66 licensed with CC BY-NC-ND 2.0.; **Page 71:** demoiselle dragonfly, David Dewsbury; **Page 72:** great crested newt, WitR/Shutterstock.com; **Page 72:** water scorpion, Bennyboymothman licensed with CC BY 2.0.; **Page 72:** water mint, edwbaker is licensed with CC BY-NC-SA 2.0.; **Page 73:** leech, d4vidbruce is licensed with CC BY-NC-ND 2.0.; **Page 73:** whirligig beetle, J. Maughn licensed with CC BY-NC 2.0.; **Page 74:** Staunton yew tree, Andy Seed; **Page 74:** Culver Oak, Paul Rutter; **Page 75:** Greater horseshoe bat, Carl Allen/Shutterstock.com; **Page 75:** bat boxes, David Priddis; **Page 75:** willow tit, Sergey Yeliseev is licensed with CC BY-NC-ND 2.0.; **Page 76:** small pearl-bordered fritillary caterpillar, Simon Colmer/Naturepl.com; **Page 76:** small pearl-bordered fritillary adult, MM-Fotos/Shutterstock.com; **Page 76:** volunteers at Ruspidge Halt, Kathy Reynolds; **Page 76:** herdwick sheep, CreativeCaptures1/Shutterstock.com; **Page 77:** highland cow, Sue Middleton; **Page 77:** Exmoor ponies, Sue Middleton; **Page 77:** lords and ladies, Picture Esk is licensed with CC BY-NC 2.0.; **Page 78:** meadow flowers, Rosie Kelsall; **Page 78:** elephant hawk moth, Odd Wellies licensed with CC BY 2.0.; **Page 78:** Crump Meadow Colliery Pond, David Dewsbury; **Page 79:** grass snake, Phil Rudlin; **Page 79:** reptiles survey, Andy Seed; **Page 79:** slow worm, Vitalii Hulai/Shutterstock.com; **Page 79:** common lizard, SADLERC1/Shutterstock.com; **Page 80:** Leoni Dawson, Leoni Dawson; **Page 80:** Kevin Caster, Kevin Caster; **Page 81:** Kate Wollen, Kate Wollen Forestry England; **Page 81:** Emily Bennett, Emily Bennett; **Page 81:** David Priddis, David Priddis; **Page 82:** Rosie Kelsall, Caroline Maggs; **Page 82:** David and Susan Dewsbury, David Dewsbury; **Page 83:** Ben Robinson, Ben Robinson; **Page 83:** Paul Rutter, Paul Rutter; **Page 84:** weasel, susie2778 licensed with CC BY-NC 2.0.; **Page 84:** pheasant, Paul Albertella licensed with CC BY 2.0.; **Page 84:** rabbit, Eric Isselee/Shutterstock.com; **Page 84:** American mink, An inspiration/Shutterstock.com; **Page 85:** Himalayan balsam, Andy Seed; **Page 85:** rhododendron flower, cdstocks/Shutterstock.com; **Page 85:** grey squirrel, IrinaK/Shutterstock.com; **Page 85:** boar damage, Sue Middleton; **Page 86:** Herdwick sheep, Helen Chick; **Page 86:** sheep with trailer, Sue Middleton; **Page 86:** tree pipit, naturalengland is licensed with CC BY-NC-ND 2.0.; **Page 87:** all leaf photos, Andy Seed; **Page 88:** all bark photos, Andy Seed; **Page 88:** hawthorn berries, Andy Seed; **Page 88:** rowan berries, Forestry Commission; **Page 89:** common vole, AgneVaitke/Shutterstock.com; **Page 89:** stoat, Derek.P. licensed with CC BY-NC-ND 2.0.; **Page 89:** common shrew, volesandfriends licensed with CC BY-NC-ND 2.0.; **Page 89:** heron, Erni/Shutterstock.com; **Page 89:** song thrush, hedera.baltica licensed with CC BY-SA 2.0.; **Page 89:** goldcrest, alh1 licensed with CC BY-NC-ND 2.0.; **Page 89:** old man's beard, ndrwfgg licensed with CC BY 2.0.; **Page 89:** bramble, David Priddis; **Page 89:** wood anemone, Bernt Rostad licensed with CC BY 2.0.; **Page 90:** Forest in spring, tom c licensed with CC BY-SA 2.0.; **Page 90:** Foxes Bridge Colliery, Dean Heritage Centre; **Page 91:** ramorum diseased tree, Forestry Commission/Yorkley; **Page 91:** large pine weevil, HWall/Shutterstock.com; **Page 92:** open space in woodland, Andrew Lebedev/Shutterstock.com; **Page 92:** sheep in Forest, Isobel Cameron; **Page 93:** orange tip female, Alex Puddephatt/Shutterstock.com; **Page 93:** Pillowell Rec, Helen Chick; **Page 94:** fly tipping, Sue Middleton; **Page 94:** harvester machine, Sue Middleton; **Page 95:** beech tree, Paul Rutter; **Page 95:** deer eating bark, Lorelinka/Shutterstock.com; **Page 96:** dead tree, Roy Pedersen/Shutterstock.com; **Page 96:** tree planting, Sue Middleton; **Page 96:** beaver dam, Sue Middleton; **Page 97:** red squirrel, Menno Schaefer/Shutterstock.com; **Page 97:** beaver, David Broadbent; **Page 97:** bluebells, kennysarmy is licensed under CC BY 20.; **Page 98:** Newt survey, Rosie Kelsall; **Page 99:** Newt trap launch, Andy Seed; **Page 104:** author photo, Andy Seed; **Page 104:** illustrator photo, Kate Sheppard; **Back cover:** Sue Middleton

Water scorpion

Wild garlic

Beaver dam

About the author

Andy Seed is the author of over 30 books, including the popular memoir series *All Teachers Great and Small* for adults, and the international bestseller *The Clue is in the Poo* for children, a guide to tracks and signs of animals. In 2015 he won the Blue Peter Book Award and is the proud owner of the show's legendary badge. Now based in the Forest, Andy spends much of his time visiting schools and festivals, inspiring children to read.

Find out more at www.andyseed.com

For details of talks for groups of all ages email andy@andyseed.com

About the illustrator

I once worked on an organic farm, where I regularly spent hours chasing escapee piglets. And as if that wasn't enough: one day when I was planting what seemed like a mile-long hedge in the driving rain I decided to become an illustrator. Since planting that beech hedge, I have illustrated lots and lots of books (including, two *Horrible Histories*, both of which are best sellers, apparently) for loads of publishers, worldwide, from here to Timbuktu (well, almost. Actually my brother rode across Africa on a motorbike to Timbuktu - and that is the honest truth.) I am also an award-winning and shortlisted illustrator...*Ta-Daaa*!

www.katesheppardillustrator.com

You might also enjoy:

THE STORY OF THE FOREST
A children's history of the Forest of Dean

Illustrated by Ursula Hurst
Andy Seed

Available from Dean Heritage Centre and online from
www.forestofdeanhistory.org.uk